AN INSUBORDINATE
LIFE

FROM COUNTRY BOY TO CANDIDATE FOR GOVERNOR

ALSO BY LOREN CULP

American Cop: Upholding the Constitution and
Defending Your Right to Bear Arms

AN INSUBORDINATE LIFE

FROM COUNTRY BOY TO CANDIDATE FOR GOVERNOR

LOREN CULP

Author of #1 Best-Selling Book **American Cop**

Published in the United States by O'Leary Publishing
www.olearypublishing.com

The views, information, or opinions expressed in this
book are solely those of the authors involved and do not
necessarily represent those of O'Leary Publishing, LLC.

ISBN: 978-1-952491-13-9 (print)
ISBN: 978-1-952491-14-6 (ebook)

Library of Congress Control Number: 2021904119

Editing by Heather Davis Desrocher
Proofreading by S.R. Boland
Cover design by Christine Dupre
Book design by Jessica Angerstein
Printed in the United States of America

This book is dedicated to two great women,
my mom Deeta and my wife Barb.
Thank you both for this journey that is my life.

Success does not just magically happen someday down the road, it is the end result of what you build upon today.

— LOREN CULP

Table of Contents

Preface

Writing this book has at times been a challenge. This included coming up with a title. This one seemed fitting, given the history I, and so many of you reading this, have with #insubordinate. If you were involved in my campaign, or followed it at all, you know it came about because our current governor said we were being insubordinate to him by having rallies. Anyone who understands the way our government is supposed to be run knows that public servants are subordinate to we, the people, so #insubordinate was perfect.

I've lived a long life; 60 years so far. It has been quite a journey up to this point, and I look forward to many more years, if the good Lord is willing. Deciding what to write about was the biggest challenge I faced. Sixty years gives me a lot of stories to choose from – some good, some not so good. Did I want to write about only the good things, or did I want to include the bad as well? I chose to include both good and bad, because that's real life. Life isn't all rainbows and unicorns, puppy dogs and kittens; in fact, it's far from it for most of us. My biggest dilemma was: how do I tell the truth and still follow the commandment of "Honor your father and your mother?" Honoring my mother is easy – she is an angel, a rock; the best mother I could have ever asked for.

It would be easy to just ignore the negative events in my life and focus on the positive, but that wouldn't be real – it would be phony. I'm not about phony. Although some of the information in this book sheds a negative light on my biological father, Rod Culp, I think it's important to honor his memory by including him. I also include this information so that anyone who is reading this that is involved in domestic violence – either as a victim or perpetrator – will know that it doesn't have to be that way, and that it shouldn't be that way. If you are a victim, remove yourself from the situation as quickly as you can and seek help from family or the authorities. If you are the perpetrator of domestic violence, then stop now and seek help.

Although we learned that our father didn't always set the best example, my brothers and I were raised to be honest men who care about the truth, and to love America and the foundation it was built on (individual freedom and liberty, the Declaration of Independence, the Constitution, the Bill of Rights, the 10 Commandments, and the Golden Rule).

We are far from perfect; I'm not perfect, no one is perfect. We all take the bits and pieces of life's experiences that make us who we are, good and bad; then, we do the best with what we are given, while fighting to make things better. In the long run, it will not matter whether you were rich or poor in money; we will all arrive at the end of this journey we call life and breathe our last breath. What will matter then is, did you make the most of it while you were still breathing? Did you love those around you the best you could? Were you rich in love, and did you help your fellow citizens? Did you work as hard as you could, or just hard enough to get by?

I decided to write this book after about 18 months of campaigning for governor of Washington state and after about 60 years of waking up every morning "sucking air." I'm not writing this to say, "Look at me," or "I'm great, read about me." I wrote this book about my life's adventures to show everyone reading it that it doesn't matter who you are or what your background is – YOU matter, and YOU can do anything you set your mind to. I hope to inspire YOU. Life has ups and downs. I've been poor living on food stamps, and I've also run a successful business.

I want everyone who reads this and supported me throughout my life and during the campaign for governor – the thousands who came to rallies, who donated, who messaged me by email or text, and even those who didn't support me – to know that I know you have it in you. You too can help effect change in whatever city or town you live in, for the good of your family, your community, and our country.

I am just a country boy and always will be. I'm sure my upbringing was very similar to that of many of you reading this. But what really matters – what really is going to effect change – is not where we came from or what we did in the past, but what we choose to do right now, today, tomorrow, and in the months and years to come. I didn't fit the mold of the typical candidate, but neither did our founders, and neither do most of you. I think you would agree – electing the typical candidate is why we are in the mess we are in right now. WE THE PEOPLE had the ability to birth this nation. WE THE PEOPLE have the ability to keep it FREE. It all depends on what we do right NOW at this very moment in time! "Let's do what we do."

CHAPTER ONE

Sometimes, You Have to Move On

I was walking down a country road as fast as I could to get home from a situation that had gotten out of control. I had several miles to go on foot, but I couldn't stay where I was. This was before cell phones, and I had gotten a ride to where I had been, so I had no way to leave other than by walking. I was walking quickly; I needed to pace myself and try to calm down. My mind was racing; I was upset.

How did this happen? Why was I in this position? My world seemed to be crashing down around me. I could only think of what I needed to do. I had to get clear of this situation and make it home to Barb, my wife of two years. We would decide what to do, together.

I had made it less than a half-mile when I heard a vehicle coming around the corner behind me. From the sound,

I could tell it was traveling at a pretty high rate of speed. I moved off the road about 10 feet. I turned to see what was going on, and my dad's truck screeched its tires and stopped in the middle of the road, blocking both lanes.

The driver's side door flew open and he got out, red-faced and angry. He was a big man; much taller, older, and heavier than I was. In an angry voice, he said, "Where the hell are you going?" I told him I was done; that I'd had enough of his crap. "I'm out!" I yelled. He closed the distance between us very quickly, leaving the truck door open, and pushed me with his full force, knocking me onto my back in the wet weeds, rocks, and brush.

He was quickly on top of me, holding me down with his weight. Both of his knees were on my arms, and he began punching me in the face. I felt rapid punches hitting me in the face and head, first from the left, and then from the right. My head was like a punching bag, moving back and forth, as the blows kept landing on the sides of my face and head. His knees pinned my arms down, so I could not protect myself or fight back. *This has to end*, I thought; *Will it ever end?* It seemed like I was losing consciousness. *He is trying to kill me*, I thought.

Then, as quickly as the attack started, it ended. I could barely see. He got in his truck and quickly drove away. I laid there for a minute or two, trying to access the damage, trying to focus. My head was pounding and my right eye was swelling so much that I could barely see out of it. I was in a mental fog. I rolled over and got on my knees as I spit blood and tried to catch my breath. I stumbled to my feet and tried to orient myself.

My legs were weak and my back hurt from the rocks and brush. I was dizzy. I sat back down. I have to get out of here, I thought; he might come back. I sat there for a few minutes accessing the damage, collecting myself and crying. I've got to get home and warn Barb, I thought; but there was no way on foot that I could make it to our house before he did – if that's where he was going. Barb was pregnant with our first son, Nick. We were both 18 years old at the time and had just begun our life together. Now, it seemed like parts of that life were falling apart as I sat there in the weeds bleeding from my mouth and head, trying to make sense of it all.

I've got to get going, I thought. I looked as far as I could see in the direction I needed to go, which was the same direction that my dad had just gone. I saw no sign of him and started toward home once again – this time, much more slowly and with tears streaming down my face.

My world was shattered. My trust for my father, who had just attacked me – and a lot had happened before this incident – was gone. I had to get home, to the one place I would feel safe. I could talk it over with Barb, and we would decide together what we would do from here. I pushed on, making sure I stayed off to the shoulder on corners where I couldn't see very far down the road. On the blind curves, I cut through the woods so I wouldn't be caught off guard again. On straight stretches, I was ready to jump in the woods and run if I saw his truck coming.

I made it about a half-mile further, where there was a large bridge over the Chehalis River that I needed to cross. The river was too wide, deep, and cold to swim in; I had to cross the bridge, but that would have left me exposed and vulnerable with no escape but to jump in the river if he came back and caught me on the bridge. I hid in the brush at the near side of the bridge, gathering the strength and courage to make a run for it. I knew he would be going back to where I'd originally left him, but I had no idea when.

My mind still whirling, I sat there in the brush just off the road for several minutes, listening intently for any sound of a vehicle approaching from the other side. The road toward town was on the other side of the bridge, but town was still miles away. Up to this point, there had been woods full of trees and brush I could have hidden in on this lightly-traveled country road. On the other side of the bridge, it was a different story. There were open fields on both sides of the road. There was no place to hide the rest of the way to Elma, Washington, the small town where Barb and I lived. If my dad returned, I could only use distance for protection by jumping the barbed-wire fence on either side. The good news was, I'd be able to see further down the road once I crossed the bridge. I could quickly run through the fields away from the road if I saw his truck approaching.

The bridge was made of concrete. There was nothing overhead; the supports were all underneath. Along each side of the bridge, running its full length, was a concrete barrier about 3 feet tall – just high enough to keep cars from driving into the ice-cold water below. But the barriers were also low enough for me to jump over, if I'd needed to escape that way. It was about 30 feet down to the river from the middle of the bridge. I could have survived such a jump; I wouldn't have fallen onto any rocks because the river was deep. But it was also very cold, and it had enough current that I could be pulled under and drown, or get hypothermia and suffer the same fate.

I was already feeling the effects of hypothermia. This was western Washington, and it's cold and wet in January. It had just begun to rain. I had been on my back in the wet, cold brush and weeds during the attack. I had walked through the wet woods part of the way to the bridge. I would be most vulnerable to another attack should I get caught part way across. I had to do it; the only other option was to walk several miles upriver to the bridge in the small community of Porter.

That option was out. I was cold and wet, and it would be dark before I made it there. My teeth were already chattering and I was beginning to shiver. I had to cross here. I had to cross now. I had to get moving. One last listen for a vehicle, and I was off. I ran as fast as I could, my back and head throbbing. I could hear nothing but my boots pounding on the concrete and the water rushing underneath the bridge. I made it to the other side and jumped into the brush.

I knelt down, concealing myself, while I caught my breath. My head was pounding with each beat of my heart, but I wasn't cold anymore. Sweat was on my forehead mixing with the now-dried blood. My breathing returned close to normal, and I started walking swiftly toward Elma, toward home, toward Barb, toward safety. I walked on, still dazed and confused, but with each step I was closer to ending this nightmare.

I made it another half-mile when I looked across the field where the road made a wide sweeping turn. I saw a vehicle coming my way; it was a little over a mile away. I kept walking, trying to see out of my eyes that were swollen from the pummeling I took earlier. Sweat, blood, and tears didn't help. I wiped my eyes with my wet shirt sleeve trying to get a clear look. I stopped as the truck came closer, now less than a half-mile from me. It was him!

I ran across the road, jumped the ditch, pushed down with both hands on the top of the barbed-wire fence, and jumped over. I ran as fast as I could. Just as I feared, I was in the open. The only thing I could think of was to put as much distance as possible between the road and me, before he got to the fence. I wasn't about to let him catch me this time. I knew his temper very well after the beating I'd just experienced. I had seen it before, but nothing as out of control as that.

I ran for 300 or 400 yards straight away from the road, looking back over my shoulder a few times as his truck approached. I was out of breath, and began to walk as his truck stopped and he got out. He hollered at me to come back. He ran to the fence and jumped over, and I took off running. He must have realized I had too much of a head start for him to catch me; I looked back to see him cross back over the fence, get in his truck and drive away.

I slowed my pace back to a walk and made a beeline across the fields to where the road met a highway. From there, it was two miles to my house. As I was making my way along the divided highway toward home, I saw Barb in our pickup, going in the other direction. I began waving my arms and shouting, trying to get her attention.

It worked. She took the exit and came across the over-pass, down the on-ramp that I had just walked on. My beautiful pregnant wife was crying as she pulled up next to me. I got in the truck – cold, wet, covered in blood, exhausted, and out of breath. I felt safe but very shaken.

I found out that she had left the house to come and look for me because my dad had gone there to take out his frustrations and anger on her. He berated her through the locked front door, telling her that everything was her fault. She had no idea what he was talking about as he hollered at her through the door, but she knew I needed her. Once he left, she got in the truck to come and find me.

Despite what I have just told you, there weren't incidents like this when I was growing up. Mom and Dad never had physical fights that my brothers or I knew about. There were some verbal arguments, as with most couples. I had a very happy, and what I would call a very normal, childhood. When I was growing up, my dad was my hero, and he taught all of us boys many things.

What led to this incident on this day? What made him do the things I just described? I walked off a job because of hostile working conditions.

Shortly after this altercation, which would not to be the last, I joined the U.S. Army. This incident was one of the many reasons for the on-again, off-again relationship I would have with my biological father for years to come. I ended up cutting all ties with him after another incident of violence, which involved the sheriff and an ambulance being called in front of my oldest son. That happened 15 years before my dad's death. I forgave my father many years ago, for my own peace of mind, but I wish I would have learned my lesson the first time and spared my son from witnessing the second incident.

My Grandpa Culp saw my dad's temper occasionally, and told me multiple times, "Never let a word come out of your mouth when you are angry." That's not always easy to do, but I have heeded his words of wisdom most of the time.

If you are in a violent situation, my advice is to get out of it now and don't look back. There are many organizations that can help; they can be found with a simple internet search. If you are in danger now, don't hesitate to call 911. No one should have to live in, or be around, a violent situation. Like I said earlier, what you have just read about wasn't what I experienced as a child. Now that that's out of the way, let's get to the fun stuff – the beginning.

CHAPTER TWO

How It All Began

I've lived freedom and liberty my entire life. I grew up wild and free – well, for the most part anyway. My parents were strict in the sense that they expected us to do what was right, no matter what, even when no one else was looking. When we failed to do that, we learned really quickly what "go cut a switch" meant, and how to "go stand in the corner" for the perfect "time out." My brothers – Randy, Kevin and Wade – and I knew what all that meant; we never wanted to hear it, but we all did.

It happened more than we wished. Those were dreaded words to hear, and we knew the result was going to be a swat across the butt . . . and it didn't feel so good. There were a couple of times that I remember going to get a switch and bringing back an old dead one that I knew would crumble easily, only to be sent back outside to find a "good one."

Culp brothers

It didn't take very many times for me to realize that I'd better keep my smart mouth shut and do what I was told, in order to not hear the words "go cut a switch" again.

Discipline is a great way to center a young man who's "wild and free," and who at times gets a little too "wild and free." My brothers and I were a little bit wild, to say the least.

Of course, we can't talk about discipline without talking about positive reinforcement when things are going right. When discipline is administered, not in anger, but by a loving parent who encourages their children most of the time, the children learn respect. Our mom especially is a very caring, loving human being. She encouraged our adventuristic side. I remember her always encouraging us to do better and to seek out the next adventure.

Baby Loren with his mom, Deeta

Our dad did the same when he was not at work, which was most of the time. He took us hunting during the season and taught us how to safely handle a gun and how to use bows and arrows. Mom taught us to use please and thank you and to say grace before meals, and she taught us that you never give up, no matter what. She showed us by her example that rain leads to sunshine, that hard times lead to good times, and that love conquers all.

I was born in Everett, Washington, on February 3, 1961 to Rodney and Deeta Culp. I remember lots of things from my childhood, including the birth of my youngest brother Wade when I was only 3 years old. Dad took me to the hospital, where I saw my mom standing in the window holding the baby in her arms.

Loren with youngest brother Wade

I remember, at 4 years old, my parents talking about I-5 being completed through the Everett and Seattle area. Prior to that, the main highway was Aurora Avenue. That's where my dad patrolled as a state trooper.

I went to kindergarten in Lynwood at Beverly Elementary, and then we moved to Marrowstone Island in Jefferson County, where I started first grade at Chimacum School. My parents bought a farm in the middle of Marrowstone Island, complete with a large barn and many outbuildings. The place had a large orchard on the right side of the house surrounded by an 8-foot-high fence to keep the deer out. The property was about 40 acres of mostly fields, but there was a small patch of timber on the left side of the house with a woodshed. We spent many hours there, stacking firewood and cutting kindling. Behind our property, beyond our back field, was a large tract of undeveloped land. There were acres and acres of woods, thick with brush and wildlife – a perfect place for us to grow up.

Loren in Kindergarten (bottom row, far right)

The house was set toward the back middle of our property, with two large hay fields on either side of the long driveway that went out to the main road. That's where we would catch the school bus to school. Marrowstone

Island has a road that pretty much goes all the way around, with a leg that goes to Fort Flagler State Park. Many times, more than I care to remember, my brothers or I would be late and we would miss the bus. Even if we were running down the driveway, the bus driver, Mr. Bunce, would not usually wait, especially after he found out we had an alternative bus stop.

One morning, we had just started to run down from the house when we saw the bus going past. Mr. Bunce didn't even stop because he didn't see us . . . or maybe he did? One of us, I can't remember who, got the idea of running through the back field and through the woods to the other side of the island, so

Loren riding Don Poncho

we could catch the bus when it came around that way. We ran with our superhero metal lunch boxes as fast as our little legs could carry us through the back field, past the barn, and through the woods to the other side. The woods were thick with brush and trees, but there was an old skidder trail that led from our barn through the woods to the road on the other side of the island. We ran to the road sweating and tired, but we were all together. Realizing we had beaten the bus, we walked to a stop where other kids, who were not as bad at being on time, were waiting. This wouldn't be the last time we would use this route to avoid getting in trouble for missing the bus.

I loved living on that farm, and I have a lot of fond memories of it. It was not without struggle, though. We all had chores to do. This was not a farm just for show; it had a purpose other than being our home. It provided us with food, along with many adventures and memories – some good, some not so good. We had dogs, cats, chickens, sheep, rabbits, ducks, turkeys, pigs, cows, horses, honeybees and one burro named Don Poncho.

You learn about the rewards of hard work when you grow up on a farm. You also learn what dirty jobs and a work ethic are all about. All of those animals – and we had many of each – depended on us for their food, water, and shelter, as well as for their protection from predators. If you are lazy and don't do your chores, the animals suffer; and none of us like to see anything suffer. We did our chores, not just because we were told to or because it was fun – which it often wasn't. But the animals depended on us, and our family depended on the food that those animals provided.

Every spring, there would be a new batch of babies on the farm – new calves, horses, and chicks. We always had new baby chicks from a hen "that went missing." The hen would show up all of a sudden, with her brood following closely behind her. There are few things cuter or softer than a newly-hatched chick.

My brothers and I didn't grow up in a rich family as far as money goes, but we grew up rich in a family bond that is as strong today as it was when we were young and figuring out life. Well, I should rephrase that. It's probably stronger today, because we don't fight each other now. As brothers, we were bonded together for life. Sometimes that bond and closeness led to fights. I am not talking about an argument, although there were many of those. I'm talking little-boy fights that rarely got too far out of hand, but they did result in broken furniture, broken bones, and broken glass.

One time, one of us hit another with a rocking chair. I can't remember who picked up the chair, but I remember all of us trying to duct-tape it back together before Mom got home. I think she noticed the tape, and it resulted in one of us cutting a switch.

Broken bones weren't something we dealt with much, but Kevin stomped on my hand one day and broke my finger; the only broken bone I've had in my life so far. It's still crooked, by the way.

Another day, Kevin and I were annoying each other as usual, and I locked him out of the house. After failing to get me to unlock the door, he punched his fist through the glass in the door and let himself in. I think it was the last day with that particular babysitter; I remember her saying, "I can't do this anymore," and we never saw her again. I told you we grew up wild and free – what did you expect?

Sometimes we would fight like dogs, but we always had each other's back when it was over, no matter what.

CHAPTER TWO

We went through some babysitters; not many of them stayed around long. I guess they didn't like "adventure." We could fight each other and then when it was over we would be fine, but if someone else tried to fight one of us they had all of us to take on. We stood up for each other. Because of that, I don't remember too many fights with other kids. Everyone knew the Culp boys were one and that the Culp boys went hard.

One night, while my parents were taking part in their bowling league in nearby Port Townsend, they dropped my two younger brothers, Kevin and Wade, and me off at the roller-skating rink. Mom and Dad taught us: "Don't start a fight, but if you are forced to fight, fight to win." I also remember my parents saying, "If someone hits you or tries to start a fight, just smile at them; don't fight unless you have to."

So, we were at the roller-rink when a boy much larger than my brother Kevin decided he was going to throw a punch. I was too far away to hear what had been said, but this boy and Kevin were face to face. All of a sudden, the kid punched Kevin in the stomach. I headed that way, along with Wade. Kevin's eyes were watering, but he was standing there smiling at this kid, and not saying a word. The boy didn't know any of us, but decided it was time to go, and he did. I'm sure to this day he is still bewildered at why he punched a kid in the stomach as hard as he could, and all the other boy did was smile back. Apparently it worked.

When we lived on the farm, Mom worked at the post office in Nordland and occasionally in Hadlock. Nordland was a general store and post office combined, and it was just a few miles from our house. My dad worked as a deputy for the Jefferson County Sheriff. With both parents working, most of the time we were "unsupervised." Even when one or both of our parents were home, we were pretty much allowed free rein on the farm as long as our chores and homework got done.

Our chores not only included caring for the animals, but household chores as well. We helped Mom out by vacuuming and assisting with laundry and the dishes. I remember a clothes washer that we had. It was electric, but it was a wringer washer that had a top-loading open tub with two rollers that you fed the clean clothes into. The rollers squeezed the water out and then we could hang the clothes outside on the line to dry.

Kevin Loren and Wade with bows and arrows

Harvest time for rhubarb

Mom always had a large garden – and when I say large, I'm talking BIG. She would assign each of us a certain number of rows to weed, often with the reward of going to the beach for a few hours if we hurried and did a good job. I remember spending a lot of time on my hands and knees getting very familiar with the dirt and weeds. It was dirty, hard work, and sometimes tedious, to make sure we pulled all of the weeds. When it was time to harvest, it was all-hands-on-deck, picking beans, cucumbers, and corn, and digging potatoes.

Mom would spend days in the kitchen, canning the fresh vegetables that we helped her pick from the garden. Sitting around the kitchen table snapping string beans, or cleaning and cutting carrots for the canner and stuffing them into quart jars, were some of the things we all learned to do.

We also made our own butter from the heavy cream that would rise to the top of the gallon jars that were full of milk from our cow. We had a butter churn, which was a large glass jug with a handle and crank on top and wooden paddles inside. We would pour the fresh cream into the jar and put the top back on, and crank away churning it. After a little while, little chunks of butter could be seen in the cream, and before too long they collected together in a big chunk that Mom would strain through cheesecloth to form a block of butter.

My older brother Randy had the worst job of all. Since he was the oldest (six years my senior) and the strongest of us, he was in charge of the milk cow. Now if you've never had a milk cow, let me clue you in. It is not an easy chore to milk a cow by hand. It's not a chore you can skip or decide to do much later. A milk cow produces a lot of milk, and it HAS to be milked twice a day – once in the morning and once in the evening – or it would be in a lot of pain. A milk cow is not something you can get and then expect to just go on vacation without making arrangements for its care. It takes planning, and someone has to milk it if you are going to be gone. Although having a milk cow is hard work, the fresh milk, cream and butter are the best.

With four boys, we went through a lot of milk, and when there was any excess it was mixed into the pigs' feed. They loved it as much as we did, and it definitely helped them – and us – grow. Each morning, that milk cow would be standing ready to be milked, and each evening, the same thing. You don't have to herd or lead a milk cow into the milking barn. They will be there waiting for you. With football practice and evening games causing a late return home, sometimes the cow got milked well after dark, but it got done. I had to milk the cow by hand for a while after Randy went off to college, but it wasn't long before Mom and Dad found an old milking machine that made it much easier to do. I remember at first that it was all I could do to carry the bucket of milk from the barn into the house. I do believe I accidently spilled more than one bucket between the milking shed and the house over the years.

Along with the domestic animals on the farm, we occasionally had a few wild creatures that called our place home. Dad usually worked nights as a deputy, and on the way home sometimes he would "acquire" animals he saw crossing the road in the headlights. We raised baby raccoons and a red fox kit, along with a full-grown raccoon that had been caught in a trap. The young ones became somewhat friendly and would allow you to pet them and feed them by hand, but the full-grown raccoon, no matter how long we had him, would try to chew your face off if given the chance. He soon escaped back into the wild, and I was as happy to see him gone as he was to go. I've said many times that if a raccoon was the size of a black bear, no one would be safe outside of their homes. They are flat-out vicious animals when they want to be.

There was always something interesting happening on the farm. The freezer was always full of pork, chicken, rabbit, and beef, along with deer and elk meat that we got while hunting. The pantry was always full of canned vegetables from the garden. We didn't need much from the grocery store, that's for sure.

I had my first experience as an entrepreneur while living on the farm on Marrowstone Island. Back in the '60s and '70s, most soft drinks came in glass bottles with a deposit included in the price. If you returned the bottle back to the store, you got the deposit money back, whether you were the person who originally bought it or not. Small bottles would get you a nickel, and some would get you a dime, but the bigger bottles

Loren

would get you 25 cents. I remember spending some days walking the ditches along the roads, collecting bottles that people had thrown out of their cars. Why they did that – other than being lazy – I don't know, but it was a way to earn extra spending money for us. Finding one of the large bottles was a big deal. Twenty-five cents back then was a lot of money for a kid. The Nordland store where Mom worked was usually where we returned the bottles, and we spent some of the money buying candy. My brothers and I would occasionally walk from the farm down to the store to pick up some things Mom needed. Picking up some bottles on the way, we always returned home with a bag of goodies as well. Like I said, we were not rich in money, but we more than made do.

My second entrepreneurial experience was in the horse business. We had a few horses that we rode bareback or with a saddle. Mine was a stallion that I got as a colt. He was born on our farm and his name was Lil' Abner, after the comic strip. He was a sorrel, and a very beautiful and proud horse. When he would run, his head was high and his tail was out straight. He had a lot of spirit.

He and I bonded like no other horse I've ever had. Maybe it had something to do with us growing up together, I don't really know, but we were very close – probably as close as a human can get to a horse. I would spend a lot of time with him, and he trusted me and I trusted him.

In fact, I loved that horse. I could walk out to the pasture and call him, and no matter how far away he was, he would come running as fast as he could. I worked with him and trained him to lift his hooves for me, and I could move all around and underneath him without any trouble. With some help from my parents and older brother Randy I trained and started riding him. Lil' Abner never once tried to buck me off. Although he danced around a little bit at first, he trusted me and never threw me off.

One day when I got home from school, I went out to the pasture and called for him, but he didn't come. His pasture area included the woods on the side of the house, so I couldn't see the entire fenced area from the gate. I started to search for him. Maybe somehow he got out and was running loose. I became frantic and called his name, to no avail. Something was definitely very wrong. Then I saw him, lying on his side at the far end of the lower field, not moving. I called out his name and ran to him as fast as I could, already knowing he wasn't OK. I knelt down by his head and put my hand on his neck. He was stiff, cold, and dead. I sat on the ground next to him and cried uncontrollably while I petted his neck and talked to him. It was devastating. I gave him one last hug through tears that were flowing like a river. My buddy, my first horse, was gone.

I was in shock and slowly made my way back to the house, crying all the way. It seemed to me at the time that my world had just crumbled around me. Why had he died; how had he died? Those are questions I never found answers to. I think I cried all night and even though I went to school the next day, every time I thought of him I would start crying.

I wanted my dad to dig a hole with his bulldozer to bury Lil' Abner on the farm, but he had other plans. I returned home from school just in time to see some men loading Lil' Abner's lifeless body into a trailer. They were from a wolf sanctuary by the town of Sequim, and Lil' Abner was going to be the wolves' food.

I was furious! Through tears, I started cussing at them as loud as I could, and told them to leave him alone and get away from him. I think they were in shock to hear some of the words coming from a young boy, but I was letting them have it with all I could think of. They stood there looking at me, not knowing what to do. Dad came out of the house and took me inside for a man-to-boy talk about life and death and cussing.

I was so angry and hurt that my best friend was going to be wolf food. Now, I get it, kind of, but at the time, it just hurt. To be honest, it still hurts, even today as I write these words. Life is about sorrow, pain, happiness, joy, and many things in between. I learned that day that nothing on the farm goes to waste.

I soon had another horse, this time a full-grown mare. I remember going to see her before we bought her, and she looked very fat. Her belly was like a large barrel. The person who sold her to us said she was bloated because she got into a shed and ate a whole bunch of oats, but that "she should be fine in a few days." My mom knew better, and made a very good deal for me for this "bloated" horse. That guy must not have been much of a horseman, or hadn't paid much attention to the mare. We took her home, and as Mom suspected, a short time later that mare gave birth to a colt.

Mom let me skip school the day the colt was born. I remember spending almost the entire day with him. He would lay in the warm spring sun and sleep a lot. I spent a lot of time next to him on the ground, petting him and getting to know him. His hooves were still soft, and his legs were very long compared to his young body. Over the months that followed, I trained him to wear a halter and walk on a lead rope.

I didn't get the chance to train him or get attached to him like I did with Lil' Abner, because we ended up moving to a new place without a pasture. We kept the horses at a friend's place for a little while, but I ended up selling them both before too long. My interests had moved from horses to dirt bikes and the $200 profit didn't hurt, either; that was a lot of money in the early '70s.

The farm is also where I learned to drive. Every summer, we had the neighbor bring his tractor over to cut and bale our hay field. I was too small to load the bales on the truck, so I learned to drive it through the fields. I was so short at the time that I had to grab the bottom of the steering wheel and push myself part way under it to push the clutch in all the way. Once it was in gear and moving, I would quickly get back on the seat so I could see where

CHAPTER TWO

I was driving. We would load up the barn with bales of hay to feed the animals during the winter.

When I was in the fourth or fifth grade, our house caught on fire. A heater was too close to some fresh paint on the walls and it ignited. We were home at the time in the living room, and I remember a large noise and seeing a blast of smoke coming out of the hallway. Mom and Dad hollered at us to get outside. As we ran out the door, I remember seeing the entire hallway from the floor to the ceiling in flames. It was a very scary sight for a young boy, and I will never forget the fear. Mom put the three of us – Kevin, Wade and I – in the car and we drove to the end of the driveway to make sure the firemen didn't miss our house.

The firefighters showed up and got the fire out. We went to spend the night at a friend's house, but early in the morning the fire reignited and our house burned to the ground. It was nothing but ashes and a foundation the next morning.

To this day, I can relate very well to anyone who loses their home to a fire. It is devastating and terrifying, even for adults, but especially for children. Family pictures, records, and many things that cannot be replaced are usually gone. With the help of some neighbors and the firemen, Dad was able to get a lot of our things out of the house. The really good news was, by the grace of God, we all escaped unharmed, and we built a new home in its place. We lived in a single-wide trailer on the property while the new house was being built with the help of our Grandpa Strom, and yes, the chores continued.

Later in life as a police K9 officer, I recalled an event from my boyhood that made me really appreciate the trainability of dogs. One of our neighbors, Fennis Stevens, ran the farm next door to ours with mostly beef cattle. He was a quiet, kind, old man. Not only did he own the farm next to us, but he also owned some property on the far side of the island, and I remember riding in his truck with him to that property multiple times. It was his hobby to train his dog in a most peculiar way. The first time that I saw the training, I was amazed. Let me explain.

He had cleared a path around his property years earlier and kept it mowed down. We walked with his dog on that path to one tree in particular, where he had his dog sit with its back to the tree. He then took his walking stick and put one end of it on his dog's head. The other end he placed on a low branch, so the stick made a bridge from the tree to the dog's head. The dog didn't move a muscle. He then put peanuts on the top of the dog's nose, and started calling in a soft voice, "Come here little fella, come on."

I looked up in the tree and saw a squirrel climbing down the tree towards us. Mr. Stevens told me to hold very still and be quiet. The squirrel climbed down and walked cautiously across the walking stick to the dog's head. It grabbed a peanut and sat on the dog's head while it ate. It munched down several peanuts that way and then scamp-ered back up the tree.

After he gave the dog a much-deserved reward, we walked to an area where he had a picnic table. He started whis-tling. He said to be still and watch. He continued to whistle, and then he sprinkled bird seed on the table and stepped back. Birds came flying in from what seemed like everywhere and began landing in the trees around us. It wasn't long before they were feasting on the tabletop.

I accompanied him to this property a couple of times, and was amazed each time by this kind old man who took the time to show a young boy what he had done. I can only imagine the time and massive amounts of patience he must have had, not only to train his dog, but also the squirrel and the birds. How many times did he have to visit that tree to get the squirrel to trust him and know that when he showed up there, it was dinner time? How trusting was his dog, to hold perfectly still while a squirrel climbed on its head and nose?

It amazes me to this day what that old gentleman had accomplished. It wasn't for any reason other than he wanted to do it. He took the time and made it happen. That is commitment! Throughout my life, whenever I thought to myself that I couldn't do something, I would remember that a farmer named Fennis Stevens trained a dog and a squirrel to have lunch together.

What can't be done? If a man can train a wild and free squirrel to climb down a tree, and to walk across a stick to a dog's nose and have lunch with the dog not minding, we should be able to do anything, don't you think? How long do you think that would take to do? I imagine an awfully long time. With consistency, patience, perseverance, and commitment, anything is possible. We just have to want it enough and make the commitment to see it through. So, the next time that you think something can't be done, just remember a farmer named Fennis Stevens, some peanuts, a squirrel, and a dog.

CHAPTER THREE
Adventure Awaits

Our summers were filled with many adventures and many opportunities. My dad not only worked as a deputy sheriff; he also owned heavy equipment. On his days off, he would clear land and dig foundations for customers. From a young age, I was not only driving trucks around the farm, but also learning to operate Dad's John Deere bulldozer, a skill that came in handy later in my life. I spent many hours as a young boy riding on the armrest of that bulldozer, watching and learning, as my dad moved dirt, brush and trees. I also spent a lot of time picking up and piling sticks and roots; always aware of my surroundings, and watchful of the bulldozer.

As a family, it seemed like we always had something going on; daily living on that farm was always an adventure, but we had others as well. We spent a lot of time fishing and hunting around the Olympic Peninsula. The many small

Fishing trip to 3 forks

creeks provided excellent fishing for small trout, and we fished around the small town of Quilcene a lot. I can still smell the fish that Mom would fry up in the kitchen, or the campfire after our fishing trips. A telescoping pole with a Colorado spinner and a worm was all we used in those small creeks. I still have my pole to this day. It was very effective; we limited out on "pan-sized" trout many times. It was a great thing to do on the weekends. Often, Mom would make a picnic lunch that we would eat on the tailgate of the pickup.

One trip we took was a pack trip with our burro, Don Poncho. We were gone for about a week into the Olympic Mountains, which are on the Olympic Peninsula – the northwest corner of Washington State. We put Don Poncho in the back of the pickup truck, loaded our gear in the car, and headed for a trailhead close to Hurricane

Ridge. Mom was driving the car and Dad was driving the truck. We all had our own packs that we had to carry, along with our fishing poles. We arrived at the trailhead and Don Poncho's pack boxes were loaded. We grabbed our backpacks which were full of small items, put our fishing poles in our hands, and headed off into the wilderness on a Forest Service trail. Keep in mind, this was the first time that either of my parents had used a pack animal, and that became apparent along the trail to our destination.

My dad was leading the way with the burro on a lead rope, and all of a sudden one of the packs on Don Poncho came off. Down the steep hillside into the timber and brush went rolls of toilet paper and other supplies. I just remember the toilet paper rolling down like someone had thrown it. Streamers of white, spreading out all over the place, bounced off of trees and rocks. Don Poncho, to his credit, stopped dead in his tracks and did not move while we dropped our packs and retrieved everything that went down the hill. A small adjustment to the straps and we were back on the trail, laughing and joking about the toilet paper.

We hiked into a shelter that was built along a creek many years before by the Civilian Conservation Corps. We camped there and went on day trips fishing around the area. The shelter was made out of small trees with three walls and a large opening facing the fire pit. It included sleeping bunks also made out of logs. The roof was made of hand-cut wooden shakes from nearby cedar trees. They all had a good covering of moss. It wasn't airtight and it wasn't very warm, but it did keep us dry. A nighttime campfire right outside the shelter was a welcome sight, and helped everyone to wind down from a busy day. We sang songs and told ghost stories. In the mornings, Mom would cook bacon, pancakes, and eggs for breakfast over the fire, and we would have fresh fish and potatoes for dinner.

We only ever took one vacation to an amusement park, and that was to Disneyland. The rest of our "vacation" time was spent camping, fishing, or hunting. I believe that is why to this day I love the great outdoors. There is nothing like it – the fresh air, the scenery, and the wildlife. Nothing compares to being one with nature and spending time in God's creation. There is a solitude and a refreshing of the mind that one experiences when we spend time in the woods. There is always a new hill to climb, or a valley to explore. You never know what you will see just over the next ridge. Just a short walk in the natural world can clear the mind and relieve stress from everyday life. We are so tied up with cell phones and social media these days that we forget about the free stuff, like a walk in the woods, the sun, the blue sky, the birds, and the squirrels – or the smells, especially after a good rain. When was the last time you took a walk in the woods, just because? We should all do it more often; I know I should.

During the summers, my younger brothers and I would spend time with our Grandma and Grandpa Strom, who lived in Anacortes. Grandpa was a self-employed commercial fisherman and Grandma was a second-grade teacher in Oak Harbor. Mom would put us on a ferry in Port Townsend, and we would be picked up on Whidbey Island by our grandparents to spend a week or two with them. The ferry rides were in and of themselves an adventure for young boys. We would stand out on the outside deck in very rough weather and have a competition to see who could stand with their feet close together without falling over as the ferry rolled back and forth in the waves.

We had many adventures with Grandma and Grandpa in the old forts like Fort Casey State Park. It was one of three forts from World War I and World War II that protected the entrance to Puget Sound from enemy ships and submarines. Known as the "triangle of fire," Fort Casey, Fort Warden, and Fort Flagler were strategically placed at the entrance to Puget Sound. They had large guns that were ready to fire 10-inch bullets on any enemy ships that might try to enter. The gun emplacements were concrete bunkers with many tunnels underneath. It made for a great place to see history and explore.

Grandma was a night owl, and more than once, we stayed up well past 1 a.m. sitting in her kitchen singing songs while she played the guitar or harmonica. Grandpa was always in bed early, and he hollered at us more than once from the bedroom when we were too loud. He was always up with the sun, having a bowl of frosted flakes. Then, he was out the door to work on his boat or mend his nets in the shed out in back of the house. Grandpa rebuilt two boats, the April Dawn and the Dawn Marie. One, I know he bought after it had caught fire and burned. He converted both into commercial fishing boats. Gill netting, crab, and later shrimp were the types of fisheries he worked.

The shrimp business is the one that took hold with my family and customers. Uncle Dan ran one boat, and Grandpa the other. They first sold the shrimp out of a pickup truck alongside the road with Aunt Donna (Mom's sister), but later bought an old gas station just north of Deception Pass Bridge on the north end of Whidbey Island. They converted it into a seafood shop or shrimp shack and an ice cream stand. I worked there one summer for Aunt Donna making banana splits and ice cream sundaes. Later, my mom and my stepdad, Jim Drovdahl, would buy the store from her. While Mom worked at the Anacortes post office, Jim ran the shrimp business very successfully for decades until his retirement.

We spent lots of time on the fishing boat with Grandma and Grandpa Strom catching crab, salmon, and shrimp. I learned to swim on these trips. My Uncle Dan taught me how to swim in a large, backwater pool on the Skagit River near Mount Vernon, far away from the swift-flowing river. I learned how to dog paddle with his help.

We also went deer hunting on Cyprus Island in the San Juan Islands, camping out on Grandpa's boat. I was no more than 11 or 12, but I usually filled more than just my tag even though it wasn't quite legal. Sometimes, Uncle Dan would take me up toward the top of the island on the Honda 90 trail bike and drop me off at a spur road to hunt by myself, with instructions to not wander too far off the old road. I had to be back at the intersection at a certain time, usually to get a ride back to the boat for lunch or dinner, depending on the time of day.

I had a lever-action Marlin .44 magnum rifle at the time, and had already gotten deer for the last three or four years. Dad did not believe in hunting with a scope, so we only had iron sights on our rifles. He said, "If you need a scope, you aren't sneaky enough." Another of his requirements was to shoot the deer in the head or neck so we didn't waste any meat.

On one particular hunt, Uncle Dan dropped me off with the usual instructions, and off he went to get someone else from the boat to take them to their place to hunt. Cyprus Island had no people living on it, but it had a great population of blacktail deer. They were small, but they were good eating. I very quietly walked along an old logging road that was almost all grass, with trees and brush along the sides. I was looking for deer and I soon found what I was looking for. As I was sneaking up the road, being as quiet as I could, I saw movement. Just off the road and up the hill about 30 yards away were three deer that had already spotted me. One was a 2-point buck. As I turned to get ready for a shot, I noticed a stranger walking up the road behind me. I pointed up the hill without saying a word, and he stopped about 100 yards or so behind me and gave me a thumbs-up. I shot the buck and it dropped in its tracks.

The man walked up, and I told him I got it. He helped me drag it down to the road, and when I told him that I had never field-dressed a deer by myself, he jumped right in and did it for me. For those of you reading this who aren't hunters, field-dressing, or gutting as we usually call it, involves removing the guts and organs from inside the animal. If you leave them in, they will make the meat unfit to eat. I thanked him and he continued on his way hunting, while I walked back to the intersection and met up with my ride. Uncle Dan and I went up to where I shot the deer, and we loaded it onto the Honda Trail 90 for the trip back to the boat. No one else in our party saw anyone hunting on the island the rest of the week, nor did anyone see any other boats or hear any shots. My chance encounter with that helpful stranger left a lasting impression on me.

Sometimes during the summer, Grandma would take me with her to college where she took courses to get ready

Loren, Kevin and Wade at Grandma Strom's Graduation

for the next year of teaching in Oak Harbor. She and I would sit in her college class, giggling about her professor. Whenever he would say the word college, he said "cawwege." Grandma had a great sense of humor and we always had a good time. Funny thing is, she never got detention for us giggling in class.

One of the most exciting parts of my time with Grandma and Grandpa was discovering bikes! There is nothing more opposite from the quiet peacefulness of nature than the rumble of motorcycles. They have been a huge part of my life from a very young age. When I was about 7 or 8 years old Uncle Dan, Mom's younger brother, taught me to ride. At the time, Uncle Dan was a young teenager and still living at home with Grandma and Grandpa Strom. He had a Honda mini-bike, and that's where

Loren riding mini bike

my love of motorcycles first started. At first, I could not touch the ground when sitting on his dirt bike, so he held onto it while I climbed on. He stabilized me as I turned the throttle and took off.

Uncle Dan had a small oval dirt track that he had built on the property, and once I got going I was fine – until it was time to stop. I would holler for him to catch me, and he would run alongside the dirt bike as I was braking to stop. He would grab onto it so I wouldn't fall over. Sometimes it worked, and sometimes it did not.

I remember walking the quarter of a mile to the gas station by the "Country Corner" and getting gas many times. Gas was only 35 cents a gallon at the time, and I went through lots of gallons on that dirt bike.

For my ninth birthday, my mom had saved her money from working at the post office and bought me a birthday present, a brand-new Honda Mini 50. It was a bright, shiny, blue bike with a black seat and chrome handlebars. My love for motorcycles was in full swing. Over the years,

Loren with his 9th Birthday Present

my brothers and I spent many days riding Trail 70s and Honda 100s. I've spent more than one day in the hospital because we didn't believe in riding slowly or being safe. We were fast and took chances. Every time we rode it was a race; full throttle or nothing. My brothers and I were very competitive, and that included when we were riding.

The Paddock kids lived on the farm next to ours and they had huge open fields of alfalfa with no fences. They all had motorbikes too. They had made trails through the alfalfa that we had to stay on, so we wouldn't tear up the crop too much. There were multiple trails with intersections; it was like a mini-highway system. Of course, we had to have rules and "cops" too. We would often play cops and robbers on dirt bikes. The "robbers" never wanted to pull over, so we devised a somewhat difficult way to catch a robber. We would ride up alongside them – sometimes at full speed – and kick the back of their motorcycle seat, causing them to crash. I don't remember anyone getting hurt too badly, but I do remember lots of broken handlebars and dented gas tanks.

Loren on his Honda 100

I did have one bad accident – not from playing cops and robbers, but from racing with my brother Kevin on the power line road. Some other family friends who lived next to the Port Townsend airport also had dirt bikes, and close to their house was a power line. We would leave their house and ride for hours on the dirt road used for power line maintenance. We rode miles away from the house on this one particular day, and on the return trip we wanted to see who would arrive back at our friends' house first.

The race was on! Kevin and I both had Honda 100s and were pretty well matched on our riding skills. We were going full-out coming around a corner on a downhill slope, and I went off the road, hit a stump, and went flying off the bike into the air and over the hill. I don't remember much after that, except a couple of flashes. I remember sitting on the ground and all of the kids on the ride that day were standing around laughing. I think they caught on pretty quickly that I wasn't OK. The next memory I have of that event was being on the back of Kevin's bike, holding on to him: then being put in Mom's car after puking on the ground. I woke up next in the hospital with Mom by my side, and I stayed overnight with a concussion. Did it slow us down? I'm not too sure about that, but we were a little more cautious – at least I was – for a day or two.

Right after I got my driver's license at 16-years-old, I took the test on one of our Honda 100s, and I've had my motorcycle endorsement and multiple motorcycles since.

There is not much that compares to off-road motorcycles. The thrill is real.

Barb and Loren on their Harley Davidson

I now prefer to "roll the power on" on the highway with the rumble of a Harley-Davidson. I'm not much for high speed anymore, but I enjoy cruising down the open road, enjoying the sights and fresh air of freedom. Nothing compares. Barb and I even took a trip to a well-known motorcycle rally in Sturgis, South Dakota. If you like motorcycles, you have to make a trip to Sturgis. We rode through some of the most beautiful country in the Black Hills of South Dakota. We also saw some great bands and very interesting people while we stayed at the Buffalo Chip campground for an entire week. We enjoyed hearing bands like Kid Rock, Ted Nugent, Lynyrd Skynyrd, Alice Cooper, and the James Gang.

Original insubordinate 2003

CHAPTER THREE

My love for motorcycles started at a very young age, and it has been one of the constants in my life. I sold my last bike, a Harley-Davidson Heritage Softail Classic, because of a few close calls with deer around Republic, but I am on a mission to buy another one, hopefully soon.

Goodbye Farm, Hello Chimacum

Our parents sold the farm, and they bought a piece of land in Chimacum, about a mile from the school on a dead-end dirt road called the Old Anderson Lake Road. The property was heavily wooded, but we went to work clearing the land and building a house. There was no power to the property in the beginning, and I remember for a while my dad cut lumber with a chainsaw in order to build the house. Ours was the first house built on that road, so we had a huge, wooded playground all around us. There were acres and acres of land, including a gravel pit that we soon turned into something Evel Knievel would have loved. We had motorcycle jumps and tracks all over the place. For close to a mile in all directions, you would not find another house.

If you walked toward the west from our house, you could go for miles without seeing another human being. We played, hunted, and explored all over that place. Not far from the house was what we called Big Rock. It was a giant rock formation that stuck out from a hillside, high above the surrounding trees. There were caves that we explored, and someone had attached a cable down the back side of the hill that allowed us to climb up to the very top, where we had a view for miles. It was an adventurous kids' playground, and we were definitely adventurous.

This new house was special because each of us still living at home (three boys) had our own bedroom. On the farm we had shared a room and slept in bunk beds for the most part, but here we were each in our own room. Our three bedrooms were on the second floor, each with our own window overlooking the backyard and garden area.

Yes, Mom insisted on having a large garden, where we once again enjoyed the "pleasure" of weeding it. We didn't have a pasture area at this house, but we still had rabbits, pigs, and chickens for food and eggs. At one end of the house, in the living room, was a large brick fireplace. Outside of that was the woodshed, where we stacked firewood and cut kindling. On both sides of the fireplace were doors that opened to the woodshed for bringing wood inside the house. It was one of our chores in the winter to keep the wood boxes inside the house full of wood and kindling for fires. During the summer, we cut wood from the many alder trees on the property. Dad would push them over with his loader and cut them up into the right size, and my brothers and I would split and haul them to the woodshed.

A friend of my parents named Jack Hensel had worked with my dad on developing some land in Lynwood when I was in kindergarten, and they had remained friends through the years. He was retired and lived in Seattle. He came to visit once and saw us cutting kindling in the woodshed. Before he left, he made a deal with my brothers and me to supply him with wood and kindling. He paid us a dollar for each small bundle of kindling that we wrapped in a strip of car tire innertube. I saved my money, and at the age of 12, I bought a used pioneer chainsaw from a friend of the family. We were in the firewood business.

My brothers and I also built our own two-story log cabin in the woods on our property; we used it as a fort. We were Kit Carson, Daniel Boone, Lewis and Clark, or anyone else we wanted to be. We would spend hours out in the woods playing "army," not having a care in the world, except to make sure the chores were done before dark.

Soon after we moved into this house, my Grandma and Grandpa Culp sold their house in Olympia and built a house next door to us. Up until then I hadn't interacted with them much; just a weekend now and then, usually around Christmas. Having them next door allowed me more time to get to know them. Both were retired from the State of Washington – Grandpa from the Department of Natural Resources (DNR) and Grandma from the Employment Security Department.

Before working at the DNR, Grandpa had worked for the Simpson Timber Company when there was no such a thing as a chainsaw. He worked in the woods using one-man and two-man hand saws and a springboard. Grandpa loved to play pool, and when they built their new house next door to us, he included a pool room. We laughed away many hours playing pool with him, even though we could barely see over the side of the table.

Grandpa and Grandma Culp

I also spent many days on Grandpa Culp's cabin cruiser that he kept docked in the marina in Port Townsend. Grandpa built that all-wood boat from scratch in his large shop when they lived in Olympia. He had every woodworking tool – both hand and elec-tric – that you could ever want in a wood shop, and he knew how to use every one of them very well.

It took him many years to build it, but it was a first-class boat. It was called the Ella May, after my Grandma. We fished together around Port Townsend for salmon and bottom fish on that boat many times. We also hunted together for quail and deer on the land all around the house. We would wake up early, and with a sandwich in our coat pocket, we would set out to find dinner.

CHAPTER FOUR

Grandpa was a happy man. I don't remember many times seeing him without a smile on his face or without a joke to tell. He worked hard all of his life, and he did his best to pass on his wisdom to this young boy.

We lived about a mile from the school, so we walked there every school day – and sometimes even on the weekends – for a quick game of basketball. In the seventh grade, I entered a spelling bee and won first place. The prize was a certificate and a small trophy with a large bumble bee on it. I was a good speller and I loved to write stories. I wrote several short stories in junior high and in my freshman year. Now I wish that I had kept them.

Growing up in a competitive family helped when it came to sports at school. We played all of them during recess. Baseball was OK, but it could get boring. Basketball was fun, but I often had two left feet; maybe that's why I can't dance very well either.

But football was my passion. I played Little League football for the Chimacum Cowboys and later played for my high school during freshman year. I mostly played as a running back and defensive linebacker. I really liked football and the challenges, the competition, the teamwork; and the hard, tough training that each practice brought. It wasn't easy, but it was very rewarding.

Game day was very special. We had to travel to Port Townsend for our games because Chimacum didn't have its own stadium. We only had practice fields. Both Mom and Dad made sure they were at all of our games. Dad often showed up in uniform because he was working. Mom could always be heard from the stands, louder than anyone else, cheering us on.

Our coach, Pete Anderson, was a tough-as-nails logger. He didn't put up with "quit" in anyone. He motivated us and instilled a can-do attitude and never-quit mentality in the team. I wasn't very big in junior high and really didn't hit a good growth spurt until my sophomore year, so even as a freshman I was small. What I didn't have in size, I made up with grit and determination.

Chimacum Cowboys Loren #47 Kevin #38 in Little League football

That wasn't the case for my older brother Randy, who had me following in his footsteps. Randy was much bigger. He was over 6 feet tall in high school, tough and strong, and well-known and well-respected as a great football player. In Chimacum, it was a custom for the senior classmen to hang out in the middle of the main hallway and harass the younger boys walking to and from class. I was spared some of that harassment because they respected (and feared) Randy, who had already graduated and was in college by the time I entered high school.

Loren #60 Freshman in Chimacum High

There was always something to do around the house. If we weren't doing chores or cutting wood, we had other work we could do, and some of it paid a little bit. My parents bought a portable sawmill and set it up close to the house.

After school, on weekends, and in the summer we helped work at that mill or on the heavy equipment that Dad always had. Dad spent a lot of time working, and we didn't see him much unless we were at work with him. As I said earlier, he worked as a deputy sheriff, but he always had things going on the side to supplement the family income.

Family photo - where is Randy?

I went to some emergency calls with him in the middle of the night. I thought it was the coolest thing ever when the blue lights and siren came on. He didn't take me with him on any calls involving violence, but there were a few accident calls that I went with him on, and one burglary call that turned out to be a homeowner arriving home early.

When my dad had land to log, I learned to buck logs and skid them to the landing. I definitely learned how to stack lumber properly as it came off the mill. We all learned from an early age that hard work is good for the body and soul – and not too bad for the wallet, either.

Nothing in life is free, and the more you know how to do, the more opportunities you'll have in tough times so you can take care of yourself. I was learning a lot about many different things that aren't taught in schools.

Welcome to Republic

My freshman year of high school, Mom and Dad decided to make a move after we took a vacation to northeastern Washington in the summer. We traveled in a pickup with a canopy on it. Let me tell you, it gets hot in eastern Washington, especially in a metal canopy on the back of a truck in the summertime. We would camp at parks along the way, and spend some time fishing and hiking.

One of the places we visited was Republic, Washington. If you have read my No. 1 best-selling book *American Cop*, you know about Republic. It is a small, picturesque mountain town surrounded by trees, mountains, and valleys. The fishing and hunting around Republic is excellent. My parents, along with two partners, Jim Thompson and Jack Egelkrout, ended up buying the lumber yard and hardware store, Hall's Lumber. It was in an old building right on the main street of Republic, Clark Avenue, one block south of Anderson's Grocery. The building is currently being turned into a museum, but back then it was full of hardware of all kinds and had a small lumber yard on the side. I worked there during the summers and after school.

The lumber area was actually too small and shortly after buying it, my parents and their partners bought some land out by Pine Grove on Creamery Road and moved the business out there. I helped my dad build a new store at that location, where it is still running, although with different owners. I not only worked summers and weekends at the lumber yard, but I also helped to build a couple houses in the Pine Grove area with my dad.

Loren and Barb side by side in yearbook had to be destiny

Loren and Kevin Republic Tigers

Going to school in Republic was much like Chimacum. Class sizes were about the same, about 30 students per class, and the school was filled with mostly country kids. We lived about four miles south of Republic, along the San Poi River. In fact, the river ran right through our property. Our house wasn't huge, but it was a two-story with a full daylight basement. The large windows on the back of the house and the full-length deck on the second story overlooked the valley where the San Poil flowed toward the south. There were lots of beaver and muskrats in the river, and side channels that the beaver and muskrat used. It was the perfect place for a young teenager who idolized Kit Carson and Daniel Boone and trailblazers

Sunniest Smile — BRENDA GUINN
LOREN CULP

Loren Republic yearbook voted Sunniest Smile

like Lewis and Clark. I had read about the fur trade in the 1800s and how it really opened up the Pacific Northwest. Trading posts and communities grew around the area because of the fur trade. Like my heroes and many people who came before me, I was soon running a trap line and a fur business, literally right in our backyard.

It was a great income for a highschool student, with beavers worth about $30 a pelt and muskrats worth about $5. I always had gas and spending money. There were so many muskrats that I would empty my traps twice a night. I would set my alarm for 1 a.m. to check my traps.

CHAPTER FIVE

Always equipped with a flashlight, rubber boots, a sack, and a .22 pistol on my hip, I would empty the traps and reset them. It usually took about an hour to check all the traps and get back to the house. I would put the night's catch in the garage, get a few more hours of sleep, and then check the traps again before heading off to school.

Keep in mind that trapping season is in the winter, and in Republic it gets very, very cold. I remember it hitting -40 degrees Fahrenheit one winter. Add to that the wind chill factor, and by the time I got back to the house, most of the time I was almost a frozen block of ice – or at least that's how it felt. After school, I would process the prior night's catch in the garage. I'd put the hides on a stretcher for further processing, which included "fleshing" them. That consisted of using a dull knife to scrape any flesh left on the hides after they were skinned. If you didn't properly remove the flesh from the hide – tedious work – and dry them properly on the stretcher, they would begin to decompose and be worthless.

Once or twice a month when my dad made the trip into Spokane to pick up supplies for his business, I would send my hides in with him to sell to the fur company. My best friend from high school, Mike Sharbono, was also trapping in the area. It's what country boys did. In fact, that's how we got to know each other.

My first year in Republic, I was in woodshop class and I was making stretching boards for muskrat hides. That drew the attention of Mike, and he asked me what I was doing. I told him that I was making stretching boards for muskrat and he told me he was trapping them too. Years later, we both had a good laugh about that exchange in shop class, because when he told me he was trapping, I thought to myself, *I'd better hurry and get more traps out before he got them all.* He told me that he had thought the same thing! Little did we know we weren't even trapping in the same area – and there were enough animals for at least 30 trappers. We are still good friends to this day, and we don't live too far from each other here in the Republic area.

Mike and I spent a lot of time together, along with our other close friend Mike Smith, usually hunting or four-wheeling in my International Scout or cruising in his Barracuda. If you found one of us, you would usually find the others. We went through many tankfuls of gas in that Scout, going up to Swan Lake or four-wheeling up to the very top of Gibraltar Mountain.

If you've ever visited Republic, you have probably seen the large number painted on the cliff face. Every year, the high school's senior class goes up to the top and paints their graduation year on the face in large numbers. It's visible for miles around Republic. That is Gibraltar Mountain, known locally as just Gibraltar.

There is a four-wheel-drive road that goes up the east side of the mountain and we made that trip multiple times. Sitting on the cliff face, you can look right down on the city of Republic and the surrounding area. I had no way of knowing it at the time, but that spot-on top of Gibraltar would serve me well years later as a narcotics detective and would assist us in taking down a major drug trafficker in the area. It's surprising what you can see from up there with a spotting scope.

For two summers in Republic, I worked for my dad building houses. It included clearing trees, running the Cat (bulldozer), doing dirt work, running the backhoe, digging water and power lines, installing foundations, framing, hanging sheetrock, putting in insulation, and doing finish work. We also did foundations for other people, as well as remodeled a house on Curlew Lake that had caught fire and partially burned.

There was also a very dark time for me in Republic. My parents went through a nasty divorce. When I say nasty, I mean it was horrible. I didn't know until later, but my dad was abusive to my mom, and he pretty much put her out on the street with nothing but my youngest brother, Wade. When they divorced, my dad lied to me and my other brother Kevin about it. It wasn't until years later that I found out the truth of what happened.

I was told a lot of lies about my mom by my dad and his lover, who soon moved in with us. I believed them at the time. Mom and Wade moved to the west side of the state, close to my grandparents, and I had little contact with them for quite some time because of the lies I was told – and naively believed. *My dad was my hero – he wouldn't lie to me,* I thought.

A broken home is no place to be. It's hard on everyone, especially the kids. I remember spending many nights with the lights off in my room, listening to music with tears streaming down my face. Usually, it was Merle Haggard and the song "Silver Wings." Why was this new woman living in our house? Why did Mom leave? What went wrong? Did I do something to cause this? These are all things that go through a young person's mind when their parents' divorce. I vowed to myself that I would never let that happen when I got married.

My dad was gone a lot, which left two teenage boys home alone. Yes, we did things we were not supposed to do, like have friends over for parties when Dad was out of town. For the most part, though, we stayed out of trouble. Football kept Kevin and me busy in the fall and winter of 1977. I loved football; the teamwork and camaraderie helped to keep my mind focused and off of family problems.

Loren age 16

CHAPTER SIX

A Young Lady Named Barb

After school I usually offered a ride to anyone who got in my Scout and asked. On one particular day, one I will never forget, my Scout filled up with the usual friends, but there was one new passenger, Barb. She sat in the middle of the back seat, in between two other people; two more were in the front seat with me. After the first stop there was an open spot in the front. I asked if anyone wanted to ride up front. I was looking in the mirror, right into Barb's eyes, and she was looking at me. As soon as I asked the question, before the last words even left my mouth, one of the other girls in the back climbed over the seat and sat in front. I looked back at Barb and I could tell she was not happy; neither was I. I looked back into those blue eyes a few times and saw them looking back at me. I later found out – and we're talking about it as I am writing this – that she was too shy to be as forward as the other girl, even though she and I were thinking the same thing. We both wanted her in the seat next to me but were each too shy to do anything about it.

I was definitely shy in high school; I'm talking, very shy. I'm still not a very outgoing person to this day, despite what you might think after the 2020 campaign. Out of the need to do what I felt I needed to do for our state and we the people, I pushed myself out of my comfort zone to speak publicly. But back to high school. There were a few girls in my class who quickly figured out how shy I was. When I would be sitting in class before it began, they would say, "Hi Loren," in unison and my face would turn beet red. They did it to me all the time. Apparently, it was fun for them to watch my face light up. I took it in stride; it was a running joke, and it made me laugh, even as my face was turning as red as Rudolph's nose.

When I first moved to Republic, Barb had a boyfriend, but during the summer of 1977 she had broken up with him. Her brother Rick Clough and I spent some time hunting and four-wheeling, and one day that summer we were going to take a trip to Swan Lake to go swimming. It was a very hot day in Republic, and Swan Lake is a popular "swimming hole" for locals. There are a lot of people who come to Republic to camp, as well. Rick said his sister Barb wanted to go, and I had no objections. In fact, I was more than happy to get to know her.

We spent the day at Swan Lake talking on the beach and swimming. I had a pretty good idea after that day that she and I had a future together. Don't ask me how I knew, but after that day I was head over heels for her, even though I didn't show it at the time. Remember, I was shy. Anytime Rick and I were going to do something, I would ask if his sister Barb wanted to come along – and many times, she did.

Barb and Loren 1977

When school started, we had become friends. We sat next to each other in a few classes, and talked even when we weren't supposed to. She was easy to talk to and easy to look at. Later in the fall after a home football game, Barb was waiting for me as I came up the hill from the field toward the locker rooms. She told me I played a good game and gave me a hug. I don't remember whether we won or lost the game, but I liked the reception from her. She asked me if I wanted to hang out at a friend's house after I got my gear off, and I said yes. I got her the keys to my Scout so she could wait in it and stay warm. I took a quick shower, and ran out the door of the locker room to her waiting in my now warmed-up Scout.

We were inseparable from that night on. A few dates later, I asked her if she would be my girlfriend, and she said yes. From then on, almost every day, I would pick her up in the morning and drive her to school, and then I would drive her back home after school. She played basketball and I played football; that is, until I got my second concussion.

It was an away game and I was playing fullback. I remember the snap of the ball, getting the handoff from the quarterback, and running through a wide-open line. I saw the end zone and I was running at full speed toward it, with nothing but TOUCHDOWN on my mind. It was a clear shot to the end zone with no defenders in my sight. The next thing I remember was laying on the ground on the sidelines behind my teammates with some people standing over me. I blacked out again and briefly woke up in an ambulance.

The next day, I woke up in the hospital and my head hurt like no other and I was sick to my stomach. My brother Randy was there and told me what happened. When I cleared the line with the ball and was running toward the end zone, two of the defending linebackers came from both sides. Their helmets smashed into mine at the same time, completely knocking me out. I was carried off the field.

When I got home from the hospital, Barb was there waiting with a stuffed teddy bear for me. She stayed by my side a lot while I was recovering. On a follow-up visit with the doctor, he told me I couldn't play football anymore because the next concussion could be my last. It wasn't worth the risk. Bruising of the brain is nothing to play with, and so, reluctantly, I took his advice.

I still showed up for practice and games, cheering on my team, but it wasn't the same ever again. Standing on the sidelines is nothing compared to being in the game. School was a means for me to play football, which I loved; now that I couldn't play, school wasn't the same. No longer could I wear a jersey with my team during school on game day; I wasn't part of the team. I felt kind of lost without football. I was now just a spectator of what once was a huge part of my life. Kevin was backup quarterback and eventually the starter, but I was gone by then and didn't get to see it. Things were changing, and I didn't like most of it.

I did, however, like the fact that Barb and I continued dating and were falling in love more and more each day. I started thinking of the future; our future together. My dad had always been very conservative, and he railed on sometimes about what was being taught in public schools. He had been a national speaker for a time when we lived in Chimacum, talking about conservative values to audiences across the nation.

Loren and Barb side by side in yearbook it had to be destiny

Loren and Barb dating

Loren and Barb at Prom

He had told me years before, "When you are 16, if you want to get your GED and go to work, you can." He spoke of the business world, and how no banker or customer had ever asked to see his college degree. In the business world, he said, they care about things like integrity, trustworthiness, and the ability to get the job done, no matter what. He had always preached about being one's own boss and not just having a J.O.B., which he said stands for "Just Over Broke." I went to him shortly after my football "career" ended for good, and told him I wanted to get my GED and go to work full time. At 17 and as a junior in high school, I took the GED tests and passed with no problem.

I went to work full-time with him to continue with my "degree" in the real world of construction and business. Soon after, he and his partners had a falling out, and he sold his share of the lumber yard to them. He and I formed a new company – we were partners! We did some remodels during that winter, and as soon as spring and summer came, we did dirt work and installed concrete foundations in and around Republic. Toward the middle of summer, things were going great, and I had moved out. I was living in my own apartment in Republic, in an old hospital that had been converted to apartments. My best friend Mike Sharbono and I shared the apartment.

My dad and I talked about either staying in Republic or moving back to the west side of the state, where we could work year-round without dealing with subzero temperatures in the winter. It's impossible to pour concrete foundations in the winter in Republic, because the concrete will freeze and fall apart. That leaves a small seasonal window to actually do the work.

Wedding pictures

The decision was made to move before the next winter. I was in agreement and was ready to go wherever he was going. but there was one problem. I wasn't going to leave Barb. "I'm going to marry her, and she is going with us," I told him. He told me that if her parents gave their permission for us to get married, then I would have his. We were both only 17, but there was no way I was leaving her behind. Barb and I talked it over with her parents, Bud and Carol, and thankfully they gave us their blessing.

We were married in the Republic Church of the Nazarene on August 5, 1978. Our honeymoon consisted of one night in the honeymoon suite in a hotel in Spokane, complete with a bottle of champagne, courtesy of the hotel (they didn't ask our age). Then it was back to Republic and work.

Barb's 18th Birthday, soon after we were married

My buddy Mike moved out of the one-bedroom apartment, and Barb moved in. Our life together had begun, and three months after we were married Barb turned 18. I did the same a couple months later. We were two young kids who didn't know what lay ahead, but we were determined to succeed in this experiment we all call life.

We moved from Republic to Grays Harbor County before the snow flew that next winter. Kevin did not move with us; he stayed to finish school with some family friends.

Goodbye Republic, Hello Elma

My dad bought a piece of land close to the Satsop River. The land didn't have a house on it, but it did have a large, old barn. We went to work improving the property, and he bought a manufactured home for it. Instead of drilling a well, we dug a huge hole at a spring on the property. Then we placed large concrete rings down in the hole and stacked them up above ground level. We filled in around the rings with washed rock. It wasn't long until the water from the spring filtered through the rock and filled the new "well." With a pump and water lines installed, we had a freshwater source for the property.

Barb and I had little money, but we were saving what we could for a down payment on our own place to live. Instead of paying rent, we decided to move into the old barn. We cleaned out the hay loft and moved into it. It was very old and smelled of dust and hay, but it was our home for a time. There was a ladder built on an interior wall that was our access up to the loft. We moved a couple of dressers and our bed in, and put an area rug on the rough wood floor.

We shared the barn with owls that roosted in the rafters, but the loft had its own ceiling – so we were never pooped on by the owls. It was definitely cold at night, and the loft didn't have a door on it, but we just piled on more blankets and snuggled to keep warm. We didn't have running water, heat, or any of the comforts that you would normally expect in a place to live, but we didn't care. We were together, young, and happy, even if our home was in the loft of an old barn and our roommates were owls. They didn't seem to mind, and we didn't either; we were free and had our whole lives in front of us. What a journey we had begun.

We saved until we finally had enough for a down payment on a new single-wide mobile home. We bought it in Olympia and had it moved to a mobile home park on Fairgrounds Road in Elma . . . our first home together.

Loren after a hard day's work

Loren relaxing in new home

I kept busy for a while working with my dad, clearing land, logging, installing foundations, and building houses. We did whatever work we could find. Jimmy Carter was president, and as the end of his first and only term drew near, the economy was tanking. Interest rates were high,

Loren Christmas 1979   *Barb Christmas 1979*

and the building industry slowed to a crawl. It became longer and longer between jobs. This didn't help my dad's already short fuse.

We were working on my Grandma and Grandpa Culp's new house in Elma when the altercation that I began this book with happened. There had been a series of conflicts before that, which had occurred partly out of frustration and partly out of working with family. We were putting the final touches on their house and doing inside trim. As my dad walked by, I asked for help in holding a long piece of wood trim that I had to cut. It was the beginning of the day, and once again he was grumpy. He continued to walk by and said, "Hold it yourself!" I'd had my fill of his anger and told him I was done. I walked out to the work truck and started it to leave. He pulled the door open and took the keys, telling me I could walk. Then he pulled me out of the truck to the ground and walked back in the house.

After the beating that followed my walk down the road (again, the details were recounted at the beginning of this book), I decided to join the U.S. Army. It was time that Barb and I were really on our own.

Our oldest son Nick was born at St. Peter's Hospital in Olympia about the time Mount St. Helens blew its top in the spring of 1980. We sold our home to my older brother Randy, and soon I was off to basic training at Fort Leonard Wood, Missouri, in the "Show-Me State." Barb and Nick stayed at her parents' house in Republic while I was in basic training.

CHAPTER EIGHT

We're in the Army Now

My very first airplane ride was courtesy of Uncle Sam. I flew from Spokane into St. Louis and then took a smaller plane to the base. Those flights began my love of flying. There was something about seeing the earth from the air that intrigued me. My seat on the first flight was in the middle, one seat away from the window. A very nice lady had the window seat, and she could tell I was eager to look out the window, probably because I was leaning over her to look out. She offered to switch, and I accepted her seat and she took mine. I think my face was glued to the window the whole flight from Spokane to St. Louis. Seeing the mountains, farmland, and cities from high above captivated me. It was very exciting, and to this day I love to fly. Years later, in the mid '90s, I would have a pilot's license.

I spent a week in-processing at Fort Leonard Wood. The barracks, where hundreds of other new recruits and I stayed, were old wooden World War II-era buildings. They were devoid of air-conditioning, and it was VERY hot in Missouri. We spent that first week getting our vaccinations, gear, and uniforms, including boots.

I've never forgotten the day we went through the uniform and boot building. There is one person who I would love to have a word with to this day, but he is probably dead and gone by now. When I got to the station where they issued us our boots, I waited in line like all the rest of the young men. When it was my time to get fitted for boots, I took a seat on the raised platform, and a civilian in charge of boots gave me a pair to try on. I put them on, but they were way too big – like at least two sizes too big. I told him, "Sir, these are way too big." He said in a gruff voice, "Shut up and wear them, next!" He gave me a dirty look as he threw me a second pair of the same size. I then moved on to the next stations and got the rest of my gear and uniform. That seemingly small thing – boots – would almost end my military career before it even got started; more on that later.

It wasn't long after getting my uniforms and gear that I was in one of three buses full of new recruits. The bus pulled up in front of the place that we would call home for the next few months. Basic training had begun. As our bus stopped in front of a row of three-story brick buildings, the door opened and our drill sergeant walked up the steps into the front of the bus. He began barking orders. Mostly what he said was "GET OFF MY BUS!!" Drill sergeants were seemingly everywhere, screaming and barking orders as we scrambled off the bus. These were orders that I didn't understand fully at the time; I was a civilian, a trainee.

No matter how fast we tried to get off the bus, it was not fast enough for the drill sergeants, and we found ourselves doing push-ups right out of the bus. There was a large pile of new recruits and duffle bags full of our newly-issued gear all around the area just outside the door. Some were in the dirt, some were on the side-walk, some were only part way out of the bus. One

Loren writing home from basic training

thing was clear – the drill sergeants were in charge, and no matter what we did, it was wrong. It took a while to get into a routine. Anyone who has been through basic training, or boot camp – as they call it in the Marines and the Navy – can tell you that it is exciting, scary, and a challenge like no other. But it's oh-so-rewarding on graduation day.

Those that make it through and become something more than a recruit experience something that not every-one gets to experience. Graduation is a day filled with pride and happiness. Getting there isn't easy, and some people don't make it. I know our company lost a few along the way. Some were injured and were recycled to the beginning. Some just didn't have what it took, and were discharged.

Every morning started off very early; we were assigned duties each day. After waking up to the drill sergeant banging on a metal trash can, we took showers, shaved, and brushed our teeth. After that, we made our bunks to military specifications, which (I'll never forget) included "hospital corners." The blanket had to be tight and the pillow placed perfectly. We were each assigned a wall locker. Everything in it had to be in its place and there were inspections almost every day. If something was out of place, not ironed or shined, it meant the wrath of the drill sergeant and more push-ups.

Everything we did was monitored and critiqued. We had little time to do the things we had to do, and that was on purpose. Steel is made stronger in heat, and putting pressure on us to get things done quickly in the heat of confusion weeded out the weak and frail. I learned quickly to pay attention to the details and listen.

The days were filled with classes – physical training (PT), road marches with heavy packs, and the rifle range. Anytime we moved, we were either running or marching in formation. It didn't take long until my feet were blistered. I mean, blistered bad.

CHAPTER EIGHT

Remember when I told you about the civilian in charge of issuing me my boots? They were two sizes too big, and my feet slipped front to back as I walked and ran in them. Blisters formed all across the bottoms of my feet until I couldn't take it anymore.

I had been told by veterans I knew prior to arriving at boot camp to keep my mouth shut, don't volunteer for anything, and never complain. I kept to that, except for this.

When my platoon drill sergeant, Sergeant Maxwell, asked if anyone had any medical problems that needed to be addressed, I raised my hand. I couldn't take it anymore. He took me into his office, and I explained what happened. I expected to get in trouble and possibly recycled back to another class, but instead he had me take my boots off.

He may have been a former medic; I didn't know and didn't ask, but he took care of the blisters on my feet. He asked why I didn't bring the boot sizing problem to him earlier, and I explained to him that I wasn't a complainer and that I thought I could make it through. The next day, I had two pairs of boots in my size, and it didn't take long for my feet to heal.

Sergeant Maxwell was a Vietnam veteran, as were all of our drill sergeants. I have great respect for him to this day, even though I've never spoken to him since leaving basic training. He was tough as nails, but very fair. He wanted us to push ourselves to the limit and beyond, because he wanted us to be the best that we could be. Hmm, that sounds like an Army slogan!

I loved the hard work and the pace. It was very demanding, but – like most things that are a challenge – also very rewarding. I was 19 years old, and after working in construction, I was in pretty good shape. That made it easier for me. Some of the recruits, you could tell, had spent a little too much time in front of the TV prior to enlisting and it was harder on them. I'm not saying it was easy for me; it was still very challenging.

I made it a point to never drop out of a run or a march like some people did. I knew in my head that once I gave in, it would be easier to drop out the next time, besides the fact that I didn't like having a drill sergeant screaming in my ear. No matter how challenging a run or march was, I didn't let the negativity find a home in my head. Always positive, always fight, never give up, never give in: warrior mentality.

After one particularly long road march, we made it back to the barracks and were dismissed until chow time. Everyone was dragging; it was a grueling march and it had lasted for hours. The only thing that most of us were thinking about was getting some rest, but I never rested until I took care of what I knew needed taking care of.

Before lying down like everyone else did, I cleaned and shined my boots. I thought nothing of it, because that's what I always had done. I hated the idea of not being prepared and ready to go whenever the drill sergeant would start barking orders at us. After my boots were shined, I collapsed on my bunk just like everyone else for a short break while we waited on chow.

When the drill sergeant blew his whistle, we all ran out front and got into formation, ready for the march to the chow hall. Our sergeant came out to the front of the formation as usual, but this time he noticed something different. I was the only one in our platoon with shined boots; everyone else's boots were covered in road dust, and it was apparently very obvious. I didn't pay any attention to it until our sergeant pointed it out to everyone and had them look. *Oh no*, I thought.

After pointing out their failure, the drill sergeant made them do push-ups while I stood there. Then, we marched to the chow hall. I got a lot of "Way to go, Culp" comments, but everyone took it in stride, and we all showed up for formation with shiny boots from then on. I was soon assigned by our drill sergeant to be the assistant squad leader. It meant extra work, but I didn't mind.

Every week, we had a PT test. It consisted of a 2-mile run, an obstacle course, pull-ups, push-ups and sit-ups. Everything was timed and scored. If you got over a certain score, you got to wear an armband as a *super soldier*. That came with one important perk – being allowed to go to the head of the chow line. When it's chow time and you are part of a company of 150 recruits, it takes a long time to get in to eat. Being at the front of the line was the place you wanted to be; at least I did.

I achieved that perk around week two of basic training, along with several others, and I made sure I didn't lose it. Every week, I pushed myself hard during the PT test. That wasn't because the chow was the best in the world ("shit on a shingle" was actually not bad, though), it was because I was starving most of the time.

In basic, we had three meals, period, that we had to eat quickly. There wasn't time for snacks or dessert, and no food was allowed in the barracks. We weren't allowed to make a run to the store or order out for pizza. It was get your chow, sit down, inhale what you could in 5 minutes, and then out the door.

Everything was controlled. I was very lean and probably weighed 175 pounds. With all of the exercising and physical punishment we were going through, we burned through calories like they weren't even there. We spent a lot of time learning drill and ceremonies, reviewing military customs, practicing how to break down an M16 and how to clean it, and shooting at the range. We had to qualify at the rifle range out to 300 meters with iron sights only, no scope.

For as long as I could remember, I had been shooting and hunting. I started with BB guns and pellet guns and then progressed to larger caliber guns for hunting elk and deer. I had helped fill the family freezer, starting at the age of 8 with my first deer, and at age 12 I with my first elk. Being around firearms was second nature. I easily qualified as an expert with both the M16 and with the hand grenade, even though we didn't use those back home for hunting. Hmm, there's an idea!

The hand grenade range was a new adventure and presented new skills to learn. The grenade range was in the woods and was about 200 yards long. It was full of different challenges. We had to advance on an *enemy position* and get within grenade-throwing distance while maintaining cover, so we didn't get *shot* by the *enemy*. The grenades had to be thrown a certain way and with accuracy; grenades have a kill radius of about 5 meters, so when we threw one it had to land and go off inside a circle at the target. Have you ever heard the phrase, "Close only counts in horseshoes and hand grenades?" That's a fact.

There were also bunkers along the course that we had to maneuver around to get into a position so that we could *cook* a grenade before throwing it in a bunker at very close range. *Cooking* a grenade consists of pulling the pin and releasing the spoon. We then had about 5 seconds before it would blow up because it had a timed

Loren's official Army photo

fuse. Once we pulled the pin and released the spoon, we

would count to three, and then throw or drop the grenade into the enemy bunker.

After graduating from basic, we transitioned to AIT, which stands for Advanced Individual Training. We were now soldiers, and AIT taught us each our specific job in the Army. We no longer had the drill sergeants treating us like new recruits. We still had the discipline you would expect in the military, but it was more relaxed and focused on our specific Military Occupational Specialty or MOS. I enlisted as a combat engineer/heavy equipment operator, specializing in operating cranes.

Every day, I would go with the others in my class to the *million-dollar hole*, which was the nickname for the large pit area where the heavy equipment classes were held. The classes were taught by civilians, many of whom were retired veterans themselves.

The job of a combat engineer also includes bridge building and demolitions. We learned how to set charges with both dynamite and C4 to blow a hole in the side of a building or to take down a bridge. C4 is a plastic explosive that comes in bricks. It's white, and pieces can be broken off of the brick and formed into or around anything. It's almost like clay, except it explodes when a blasting cap is detonated inside of it. We also learned that a small piece of C4 can be lit on fire and used to heat C-rations. Our training even included how to set, detect and disarm landmines.

I almost lost a finger during training one day, not because of working with explosives, but because my wedding ring got caught on the metal deck of a crane as I jumped to the ground. My ring cut my finger through to the bone. My finger swelled up so much that they almost had to cut my ring off, but with much tugging and pulling, they got it off. With a few stitches, I was right back at it, but I rarely wear a wedding ring even to this day because of that experience.

I studied hard in AIT learning the angles, weight limits, rigging, explosives, and everything my job entailed, including the safe operation of a crane. I received very high scores in all of the requirements, and was the honor graduate of my class.

Fellow soldier and Loren

Just prior to graduation, we were allowed more freedom. That freedom included being allowed to go to the bowling alley on base during our days off. Even though I was only 19 years old, a cold beer and some "real" food, along with some bowling, helped me to unwind. The Army in 1980 didn't have a drinking age on base. If you wore the uniform, you were of age. But some people took that policy to the extreme, and there was one incident that could have gotten me into trouble if I hadn't had a drill sergeant who believed in self-defense.

There was one guy in my platoon who could never keep his mouth shut. You know the guy; everyone knows someone like that. He was always in trouble, nothing big, just a pain in the rear. He was the guy who always pushes the limits, has to be the center of attention, has to harass other people, and is just a jerk. He caught the attention of the drill sergeants from day one. He was always getting dropped for push-ups.

One night, the guy and his partner in crime had gone to the bowling alley to have a few beers. On the way back to the barracks, they stole a pumpkin from the front of the post exchange store (PX) and carried it back with them. I was assistant squad leader, so I was in a room that I shared with my squad leader. It was down a hallway, away from the open barracks where everyone else slept in bunk beds. When he got to the barracks, he rolled the pumpkin down the hall and it split open, dumping its contents at my door. They were laughing and hollering as they did it, and I woke up.

I walked to the door and saw the dead pumpkin with its guts all over the floor. I told them to clean it up as I walked to the bathroom down the hall. The troublemaker followed me into the bathroom, trying to pick a fight with me. He was hollering and putting his hands up in front of my face, wiggling his fingers like the Wicked Witch of the West. I warned him many times, probably too many, but I knew what could happen if I got into a fight. I didn't want any trouble and I for sure didn't want to get kicked out of the Army for fighting. I had a wife and a newborn baby back home depending on me.

All the commotion drew a crowd, as his loud, drunken voice woke up more and more people. I tried to move to his side to get around him, and each time he jumped in front of me and put his hands back up in my face. He wasn't going to let me out of the bathroom, which had become filled with ten other people.

After several minutes of trying to get him to leave me alone, I had reached my limit. I had taken all that I could of his beer breath, threats, and taunting. I told him to leave me alone or he was going to regret it. That just elevated his aggression. *Here we go*, I thought to myself. Now keep in mind, I'm very slow to anger and can tolerate a lot, but I realized there was only one way this was going to end. It's kind of ironic that many years into the future, my police academy class motto would be "Strike First, Strike Fast, Strike Hard."

That's just what I did. I quickly reached up and grabbed both of his shoulders with my hands. I pulled him forward and gave him a hard knee to the stomach, and then I started punching him in the face as fast as I could. It caught him by surprise, which is exactly what I intended. All he could do was back up and throw some wild punches, with very few hitting me. As he backed up, swinging his fists wildly, I stepped forward, landing more punches. We made a half-circle around the latrine and I was giving it all I had – some blows landing, some missing. He finally turned away from me and said, "OK, OK." He'd had enough. He went down on his knees, blood gushing from his nose. Then, like a spoiled little kid, he said, "I'm going to tell the drill sergeant and you are going to get kicked out of the Army!"

As I exited the latrine, I got pats on the back and "Way to go, Culp." This guy was a bully, and he had bullied a lot of people. He was a skinny 6'1" and thought he was "the man." I had put up with his heckling many times, as my classmates had, but tonight was a little different. I went back to my room, but didn't sleep the rest of the night. I wanted to make sure he didn't jump me while I was sleeping, but I also knew I might be facing the drill sergeant in the morning.

There is a CQ (Charge of Quarters) who is in charge of the barracks all through the night. This is usually a junior NCO (noncommissioned officer), or sergeant. The CQ is someone who is assigned to the company and is usually waiting to go to drill sergeant school or has just graduated. The CQ usually stayed in the office downstairs in our three-story barracks, only coming upstairs to make his rounds once an hour or so. Thankfully, he didn't show up during the fight; and apparently he didn't hear it, or he would have run up the stairs.

The next morning, true to his word, the bully told the drill sergeant that I had beat him up. With his black eye and still partially bloody nose, he marched right up to the drill sergeant and went on about how I attacked him, and that I should be kicked out of the Army. Drill Sergeant Maxwell was a short man, made of solid muscle, with a very thick mustache. His drill sergeant "trooper hat" was always present, along with a whistle hanging out of his left front pocket. As I've mentioned, he was a tough Vietnam vet, and he didn't put up with any monkey business, but I knew he was fair. I don't know that I ever saw him smile until graduation.

I was quickly called into the drill sergeant's office. I stood at attention in front of his desk: eyes forward, heels together, back straight, chest out, arms at the sides with fingers curled, thumb to the front touching the seam on my fatigues – just like I had been taught.

The position of attention is used to show respect for higher-ranking people; it's also the position that a squad, platoon, company, or larger formation is called to just prior to marching. Everything is formal in the military, especially when you are a recruit. You never want to lose your military bearing, particularly when you are in the process of being disciplined.

As the sergeant sat at his desk, he barked, "Go shut the door!" I quickly did as he commanded and returned to the front of his desk, back at the position of attention. My heart was pounding as he sat there, saying nothing. His hat, low on his forehead, hid his eyes. I was staring straight over his head at the wall, only taking a quick glance down to see what he was doing. He sat there for what seemed like eternity.

He took a couple of deep breaths and then his hat slowly tipped up. In a very stern but quiet voice, he asked me to tell him my side of the events from the previous night. I gave him as much detail as I could. After I finished telling him, he said, "Get out of my office." With a quick "Yes Sergeant!" I briskly marched to the door and quietly shut it behind me. I was very relieved, because I knew Sergeant Maxwell had a clear picture of what had happened, and he was, correctly, not buying what the other recruit told him. During my presentation of the facts, Sergeant Maxwell had asked for the names of the witnesses, which I gave him. One by one, they were called into his office.

Many years later as a police officer doing investigations, I often thought back to this day as the first official government investigation I was involved in. I was glad that Sergeant Maxwell did a thorough investigation. I, like most everyone else, never want an innocent person arrested, and I was definitely innocent of starting this fight. I threw the first punch, but I didn't start it. All I could do at this point was trust the system, my fellow recruits, and the "judge, jury and executioner," Sergeant Maxwell. He interviewed some of the recruits who witnessed the fight, and just after the last one quietly exited, shutting the door on his way out, the door flew open. Sergeant Maxwell yelled the name of the recruit who had started the fight. Then, he finished that off with, "Get your ass in here!"

CHAPTER EIGHT

Everyone in the barracks could hear what happened next. Sergeant Maxwell went off. He let it all fly. He was in the full-on drill sergeant mode that we often see portrayed in the movies. He was two inches from the recruit's ear, screaming obscenities at the top of his lungs. That's what was going down in there.

I remember some but not all of what was said. The recruit was told, among other things, that if he so much as blinked his eye wrong, he was out of "this man's Army." "I want you to keep your mouth shut and get your head into the reason you are here! One more incident and I don't care how big or small, you are gone! Do you understand that, recruit? Remove your ass from my office, NOW! Tell Private Culp I want to talk to him."

I had heard Sergeant Maxwell and was already walking to his office as the other recruit walked up to me with both of his hands behind his back. He slightly bowed as he told me in a very kind voice, "The sergeant would like to speak with you."

I entered the office, shutting the door behind me. Then, I assumed the position of attention, and announced myself at the front of his desk where he was still sitting. He gave me the *at ease* command, which meant I could be in a more relaxed stance. He told me to take a seat, which I did. He asked if I was fine with no further disciplinary action being taken, and I told him yes. He said, "From the looks of him, you disciplined him pretty well anyway, and he deserved it. If he so much as looks at you wrong, I want to know about it." He added, sternly, "I do not want any more fights in my barracks, understand?" I answered with a "Yes, Sergeant," and then – I'll never forget it – as he released me to leave, he said, "Unless it's self-defense." I turned and smiled as I said, "Yes, Sergeant." He said, "Now get out!"

From that day on, I never had one problem with that other recruit. In fact, at our graduation, that recruit came up to me and wished me the best. We shook hands, and to this day some 41 years later, we haven't seen each other. I just assume he landed in prison . . . or not.

I think that little incident helped us both, at least at the time. He probably realized that just because he was bigger than most of us, it didn't always work in his favor; and, "don't pick a fight with Culp when you're drunk."

I learned – although I had done it as a kid – that standing up for yourself, even when you are the underdog, is always important and empowering. I also learned that there is justice in this world. You just have to have the right person looking into the facts; someone who cares about truth and justice being done.

About a week before graduation, I was called into the drill sergeant's office. Sergeant Maxwell said that he had recommended to the senior drill sergeant and company commander that I go to the Drill Corporal School and become a drill corporal. During my time as a recruit on base, I had seen some drill corporals; most were not very friendly. They were young, as I was, and always maintained their military bearing. Their boots were shined and uniforms pressed. They did not wear the drill sergeant "Smokey the Bear" hat, but they had the trademark whistle hanging from their left front pocket like all the drill sergeants did. Our company did not have a drill corporal; all of our instructors were sergeants, ranging in rank from E-5 (sergeant) to E-8 (master sergeant).

Sergeant Maxwell told me that I would have to stay at Fort Leonard Wood several months longer to graduate from the school and work at my assigned company – whatever company that would be – to help train new recruits. He said that after graduating from the Drill Corporal School I would be made a corporal; he strongly suggested I do it.

Wow! To be chosen out of 150 other recruits was an honor. I didn't even know that it was a possibility. What I did know was that Barb was getting ready for me to fly home and then bring her, our household things, and our new baby Nick to my next duty station, Fort Campbell, Kentucky. Fort Campbell was the home of the 101st Airborne Division. That was OUR plan; we needed to be together. I missed them horribly after three months. Remember, this was before the internet, cell phones, email, Skype and FaceTime.

We had spent many hours writing letters to each other and making as many phone calls as we could afford, which weren't many. I was only making $460 per month. We talked a lot about graduation and then moving to Tennessee (Fort

Campbell, Kentucky, is actually on both sides of the Kentucky-Tennessee border). It was to happen in just days.

I stood there hearing the words from my drill sergeant, including: "This will be excellent for your career," "Not many people get chosen," and "You have proven yourself." I was excited about this new opportunity, but my heart was breaking. Several more months here at Fort Leonard Wood and being away from my family? I couldn't bear the thought, and I knew Barb wasn't going to like it one bit. She was home with a new baby.

All of a sudden, my drill sergeant said, "Culp! Are you in or out?" I told him that I was very happy to be put in for the position, and thanked him. It was awkward for me, and I didn't know what his reaction was going to be, but I said, "I need to call my wife and talk to her about it, Sergeant." He looked right at me and his head moved forward. He said in a calm, low voice, "Go call her," and pointed at the door.

There was a pay phone right outside his door on the wall. We were only allowed to use it at certain times of the day or night. Other times, with permission only. For those of you who are of the digital age, this might sound funny, but I picked up the phone, which was attached to the wall by a 2-foot-long cord, dialed zero for the operator, and told her I wanted to make a collect call. Then I gave her the number. My, how cell phones have changed things.

A minute or so later, Barb was on the phone. I told her the news, and her reaction was totally expected. She didn't want us to be apart any longer than what we had already planned. It was already too long, and she missed me terribly; and I, her. After telling her the benefits of being promoted, the training, everything, she said, "Well, we are coming down there, we can find a place, anyplace, it doesn't matter."

I told her I couldn't take leave and come home to get her, and then drive back across the United States to Fort Leonard Wood. I had to start the Drill Corporal School right after I was done with AIT. She said, "I don't care, we will figure it out, but we are coming. Don't worry about us, do the drill school thingy, I'll figure it out, but we will see you soon."

That was my Barb; I loved her then, and love her more now after 43 years of marriage. To this day, we are still the same about being apart. We both hate it. After a day or two apart, we miss each other terribly and are on the phone multiple times a day, talking about anything and everything. Just a few minutes of hearing each other's voices is all it takes. Little did we know that this brief three months apart for basic training and AIT would be nothing compared to what lay ahead, less than three years in the future.

True to her word, Barb arrived at Fort Leonard Wood just prior to my graduation. Her family helped out in a big way. Her dad, Bud Clough, loaned us his pickup. Her brother Rick drove the pickup, loaded down with our belongings and minimal furniture, to Missouri. Rick, his wife Sharon, and Barb made the trip with two newborn babies. Not only did Barb and I have a new baby, but so did they. The two babies were in car seats in the back of our car; Sharon took care of them from the front passenger seat while Barb drove. They drove almost straight through from Republic to Missouri, only stopping for one night in a motel. That is dedication!

I will never forget the day that Barb arrived. The sun was shining, and the sky was a beautiful blue, just like her eyes. I was in my last week of training and looking forward to graduation in a couple days and then Drill Corporal School. I had just sat down in the chow hall to have lunch when one of my fellow trainees came running into the chow hall, which was filled with a hundred or so other recruits. He hollered, "Culp, where's Culp?" I stood up and let him know where I was, and from across the chow hall he yelled, "Your wife is outside; damn, she's HOT!" I left my lunch on the table and ran outside.

There she was, the love of my life, looking as beautiful as ever. Her long blonde hair was shining in the midday sun as I ran to her (cue the romantic music). Although she had just had a baby a few months earlier, you couldn't tell. Her bell-bottom blue jeans fit her like they always had. She was so beautiful, and a sight for my sore eyes. We hugged each other tightly. A lot of my fellow recruits, who had been away from their families for months just like I had been, were lining the windows on the side of the chow hall looking out at us – or more probably, her.

There were several whistles and cheers coming from the open windows.

I took Barb's hand as we laughed at the attention she was getting. We walked along the sidewalk between the chow hall and the barracks to find some privacy. We hugged some more as tears were falling down both of our faces. Being back together made us feel whole again. Other than the day we were married, this was one of the best days in our life together. Then, as I was hugging her, I noticed the drill sergeants looking out the windows at us from their break room in the barracks. "Let's walk," I said, as I took her hand again. When she asked what was wrong, I told her, "I don't want my drill sergeant to see me cry; that would be awkward."

A day or two before she arrived, I had rented us a single-wide trailer to live in, just off base. It was very small, very old, and very full of cockroaches, but it's what we could afford and what was available. Being together was all that mattered. Barb came to my graduation with our baby Nick. It was a proud day for me to know that my wife and son were in the

Barb

stands on the parade grounds as I marched in with my company and was named the honor graduate of my class of combat engineers. I was now a trained United States soldier and a happy dad and husband.

CHAPTER NINE
Drill Corporal

I started Drill Corporal School a couple of days later. The environment was entirely different from basic training. We were now U.S. Army soldiers, and although a senior drill sergeant taught the class, it was a slightly more relaxed type of training. We learned how to be a drill corporal, a leader, an instructor, a teacher, a mentor, and sometimes a pain in the ass. We memorize how to conduct a class on everything necessary to turn civilians into soldiers.

Everything was broken down into blocks of instruction, and there were many blocks we had to know in order to pass. We learned the proper way to administer discipline, and how to teach a new recruit to stand at the positions of attention and parade rest. We learned to teach recruits how to salute and how to march. We learned commands for moving a large unit of soldiers, and the words for singing cadence. It was intense training with long hours, but It was intense for a reason.

We understood that drill sergeants and drill corporals were responsible for our nation's defense from the very beginning of a soldier's career. If we put out an inferior *product* and failed to weed out the people who didn't belong – the weak in body or spirit – then we did a disservice to our country, our fellow soldiers, and the taxpayers. We had to set a good example as well. Our boots had to always have a high shine. Our uniform had to be clean and pressed and neat at all times. Our hair had to be cut short and our hat had to always be in the right place – low on the forehead and straight forward. The whistle that we wore had to hang from our left shirt pocket (never the right) exactly so; not too low and not too high.

After graduating from Drill Corporal School, I was assigned to a combat engineer training company on the other side of the base. I was joining a unit that was already in progress and had already completed a few weeks of training.

I remember the day I showed up like it was yesterday. The drill sergeant in charge of the company threw me in front of the wolves on day one. After I reported to him, he welcomed me to the company and then said, "Follow me." We walked outside, where the company was already waiting in formation. He walked to the front and introduced me, and then said, "Corporal Culp has a few words he would like to say." I did? I was not prepared for this. They didn't say anything about this in training. I was ready to give a block of instruction on doing a proper pushup or how to salute, but nobody told me I would have to give a speech. Cold, with no prep? Oh Lord.

I swallowed the lump in my throat, and stepped to the front of the formation as my face started to turn red. It suddenly felt really hot outside. I remember telling the recruits that I was there to help them with their training in any way that I could, and that if they had problems or wanted to work on anything at all, that I was there to help them succeed. All they had to do was ask. I felt like I was holding my breath the entire time.

I turned it back over to the drill sergeant, and everyone continued with training. That's how my first speech in front of a large audience happened. Thankfully, it went OK; they were a captive audience, after all. It's not like they could ask for their money back, or throw rotten tomatoes.

My time as a drill corporal was very rewarding, because I helped people make it through the training that I had just gone through. I put my all into it. Although I was told by the senior drill sergeant that I didn't have to come in early for PT (physical training) every day, I did it anyway. Almost every morning at 5 a.m., I was on the raised square wooden platform in front of 150 trainees leading them in PT, and then singing cadence with them on a company run before breakfast. We sang cadences like, "In Her Hair She Wore a Yellow Ribbon," "A Yellow Bird With a Yellow

Bill," and "Rock Steady" while marching and running to the beat of 300 combat boots hitting the pavement in unison. To hear what it was like, search videos on the internet for "US Army cadence" or those specific titles. There are a lot of videos available.

We mixed in some swear words for effect in most of the songs. If you want your heart to fill up with patriotism, spend some time on a military training base before the sun comes up in the morning. The air is crisp and filled with soldiers and trainees marching and singing cadence. Seeing it in the movies isn't the same. Each night, after dinner in the chow hall, when the trainees were getting ready to sleep for the night, I went home. They were long days for sure, sometimes 14 to 16 hours on base, but it was so rewarding. I was helping to train American soldiers, the heart and soul of the greatest military force in the history of the world, and I will never forget my time there.

When I got my orders to head to my original duty station, Fort Campbell, Kentucky, I had mixed feelings. I didn't want to leave; I loved what I was doing. But Uncle Sam said pack up and move out, so that's what we did. My time as a drill corporal was coming to an end, but my new adventure as a member of the legendary 101st Airborne Division (Air Assault) was about to begin. I received many letters of commendation from my commanders at Fort Leonard Wood for the work I had done there. We loaded up a U-Haul and headed to Fort Campbell.

CHAPTER TEN

Air Assault!

Fort Campbell straddles the Kentucky-Tennessee border. We moved into a single-wide trailer on a half-acre in Clarksville, Tennessee, just a few miles from the base. Times were hard financially, but we made do. I was making a little bit more than the $400 to $500 a month that I made before, but not by much. We were receiving a housing allowance now, along with a small portion for *rations*. Barb and I gave blood every chance we could, too, and the extra $20 they paid helped out.

Every month after payday, we treated ourselves to a meal out. We went to the local McDonald's, where Nick had a Happy Meal. Barb and I had Quarter Pounders with cheese and shared a large fry and a Coke. It was not much, but it was our *luxury* spending for the month. Nothing like living the high life!

Barb at the entrance to our mansion

There were a couple times toward the end of the month when there wasn't any money left. I'm talking about none. One night after the babies were fed, we looked at each other as Barb was heating up a can of string beans for dinner, and laughed. It was literally the last thing in the house, other than baby food, that was edible. The cupboards were bare, and so was the refrigerator. If payday wasn't the very next day, we could have survived on cockroach stew; there were plenty of them.

I was assigned to B Company, 426th S&S Battalion. B Company, or Bravo Bulls as we were called, was a forward support company. We kept the forward units – aviation, artillery, and infantry – supplied with everything they needed, from bullets to beans and everything in between. I was assigned to the heavy equipment section as an operator, where we moved lots of ammo, missiles, rations, and fuel.

The military is all about training, and we did lots of it. It seemed like our unit spent more time in the field training than it did in the garrison. We all spent extended time away from our families. We were part of the Rapid

Deployment Force, subject to being called up at any moment. We never knew where we were going until we were airborne with all of our equipment and supplies. When deployed, we would fly in large cargo aircraft supplied by the U.S. Air Force. The 101st Airborne, and other U.S. units that were part of the deployment force, had to maintain mission readiness and have the capability of being anywhere in the world within 48 hours.

Thankfully, under President Reagan's peace through strength policy, none of us spent any time in war. Many of our missions were to the woods of Tennessee, but we also flew out to Texas and Puerto Rico, where we had war games involving every branch of the military. I was quickly promoted to acting sergeant, and soon found myself in charge of the heavy equipment and the heavy equipment operators in our company. Once again, I was in a leadership position with the responsibility for equipment and people. I loved it because I loved the challenge. Leading people from all walks of life, backgrounds, and upbringing can be challenging at times, but we were a very tight unit. We took a lot of pride in our work and mission.

Right down the road from my company headquarters was the original Air Assault School. It was known as the "toughest 10 days in the Army." It lived up to that name. Once you graduated from Air Assault School, you were issued the Air Assault badge, which you wore pinned to your uniform from that day forward. Everyone knew that if you were wearing that badge, you endured hell on earth to get it. Every day, I would drive from the company headquarters to the motor pool where our equipment was kept and pass by the Air Assault School.

It wasn't long until I was a graduate. It was intense physical and mental training, night and day, for 10 days. This was no gentlemen's school; the instructors were like drill sergeants on steroids. No one who went into the class wore any rank, even officers. We were all treated the same, like a lowly day-one recruit. We only knew the others' ranks on graduation day.

Aside from the grueling physical part of the training, we learned how to rappel out of helicopters and down the sides of a building on ropes to enter through a window, or continue on to the ground. We also learned how to rig vehicles and pallets of equipment and supplies to be airlifted. If you've never been smacked in the head by a helicopter creating hurricane-force winds, hovering just above you while you are trying to hook up a load or discharge the static electricity that helicopters generate so you are not

Air Assault

shocked or knocked over, then you haven't lived. The day they pinned that badge on my chest was a very proud day.

CHAPTER TEN

Sometime after graduating from Air Assault School, I was selected by my first sergeant, Sergeant Chapman, to attend Rappel Master School with him and my company commander, Captain Hampton. In this class we learned to rig up ropes to a helicopter and be the person in charge of the troops in it. We had to make sure that everyone was rigged up correctly with their harnesses and that the ropes were secured. We communicated through headsets in our helmets with the pilots inside the helicopter. If we messed up or didn't catch a problem with either the rigging of the ropes to the helicopter or the rigging on the troops, someone could fall over 100 feet and die. No pressure.

It was intense, it was loud, it was one of the greatest thrills ever, and thankfully nobody died. We also did something called STABO. This is an extraction technique used to remove a small unit of troops quickly. Roller coasters and carnival rides have nothing on the thrill I experienced doing this. You can watch short videos on this by searching "US Army STABO" on the internet.

I was very thankful that First Sergeant Chapman selected me to attend the Rappel Master School with him and our commander. Both men were Vietnam veterans and true warriors. I came to know Sergeant Chapman pretty well. As most people who have served in the Army know, the First Sergeant is called "Top" because they are the top sergeant in the company. I worked closely with Top, as did most of the NCOs in our unit. He was a mentor to me, and taught me what a real leader is all about. He had the respect and admiration of everyone. He was the epitome of a lean, mean, fighting machine, and he lived it every day. When we went on company runs, everyone wore T-shirts, shorts, and running shoes – but not TOP. He always showed up in a T-shirt, shorts, and *combat boots.* He did not hesitate to get on your ass when you screwed up, but he also didn't hesitate to give you a pat on the back when you did a good job.

I witnessed him going without sleep for multiple days on several occasions during deployments so he could make sure his troops were taken care of. He taught me so much about what a real leader is – not just by his words, but by his actions as well. In life, you can command respect just by the rank you wear on your uniform or by your position; but to GAIN respect, whether it's in the military or in civilian life, you have to EARN it through your words and actions. Top did both, and I will be forever grateful for his mentorship and the example he set for me and the others who were stationed with him and who served under him, in the world-famous 101st. His leadership, his example, changed my life forever.

He encouraged me to go into the leadership school, the Noncommissioned Officer Academy, at Fort Campbell. He was a very proud dad the day I graduated as an honor graduate of my class. Just recently, through an old Army buddy of mine, Troy Arnett, I was able to reconnect with "Top" Larry Chapman on Facebook. He is now a church pastor, serving his church in Mexico. After all of these years, he still holds a special place in my *Insubordinate Life*, and he always will.

I loved most things about being in the military . . . I said, most. I actually wanted to make a career out of it. In 1983, I received orders to go overseas to South Korea. We now had two little boys; Adam was born in the hospital in Clarksville, Tennessee, in November 1981.

Family photo Tennessee

Going to South Korea was going to be another adventure. The only problem was, I had to go alone. My family could not accompany me because I was going to the 2nd Infantry Division, stationed close to the Demilitarized Zone (DMZ). That is the border between South Korea and the communist North. It was too dangerous for family; they had to stay home. The thought of this much time apart was rough, and going through it was even rougher than we could have imagined.

Loren and Nick Tennessee

For one whole year, I was apart from Barb, Nick and Adam. Nick was almost three and Adam was one when I left. Remember, this was 1983. It was before the internet. It was before cell phones, emails, and video chats. I kept in touch the old-fashioned way, through handwritten letters and through our once-a-month phone call made possible by the USO.

It was heart-wrenching and painful, to say the least. Even to this day, as I type out these words, I'm tearing up. I'm glad this isn't a video. The pain of not being with your family, not holding them, not being able to comfort them or see them, was almost too much to bear for all of us. Nick, who was my little buddy and always ran to the door to greet me when I got home every night, was without me and I him. Adam was just a baby in diapers; we didn't even have much time to bond before I left.

Barb, who I love to this day with all my heart, was left alone to raise our boys and take care of everything at home. Just as we were getting ready to drive home to Washington before I left for Korea, a deployment came down. Change of plans. We quickly bought plane tickets and Barb flew home to Spokane with the two babies, where her family picked her and the boys up. After the deployment, I drove back to Republic before flying out to Korea.

I know she often felt helpless and abandoned. Life is tough as it is, but it's even tougher away from the ones you love. We endured, as many military families do when their families are split apart by deployments. What else is there to do but suffer through it and complete the mission? It's what we signed up for, kind of. While in Korea, I was promoted to sergeant; not having family there to witness it stung, but I will never forget the homecoming.

The people of Korea were very appreciative of us being there. I worked with many civilians assigned to our unit on base, and they were some of the kindest people I have ever met. A couple of times I was invited to their homes for dinner with their families.

I also participated in a joint military exercise called Team Spirit. Every branch of the U.S. military and Korean forces was involved, and it took place all across the country.

My company would travel from one place to another in long convoys of jeeps, trucks, and equipment. Scattered around the countryside on dirt roads were small villages that our convoy would pass through. Whenever the people who lived there heard our convoy coming, they all ran to greet us. Children and adults lined both sides of the road; they would wave to us with one hand, and hold small American flags in the other. They all had smiles on their faces as we passed. I will never forget that experience as long as I live. It made me very proud to be an American.

One of my extra duties was serving as the company field sanitation NCO. Whenever we were in the field, I was in charge of field sanitation. When we were in garrison, I had to make sure I had every supply we might need, in order and stocked. What does that entail in the field, you might ask? Well, among the other things in garrison, being in the field brought on a whole new meaning. During Team Spirit, which was in the bitter cold of a Korean winter, I had to make sure that everyone had a place to take a dump. Prior to deploying, I built some darn fine latrines. They were the most comfortable seats the Army has ever seen.

Oh, I'm laughing as I write this. At the end of each day, my *volunteers* would empty out the lined trash cans under the seats, and we would go up on a hill. As I supervised them, they would stir and burn the contents with diesel fuel in a 55-gallon drum cut in half. With snow on the ground and a wind chill probably sub-zero, it didn't take long until I had more volunteers than I needed. The job was a pretty smelly one, but it was warmer than standing in a frozen foxhole. I wish I had pictures!

After an entire year, I arrived back in Republic late on a snowy night in January. I walked in the front door of the duplex that Barb and the boys were staying in. The boys were asleep in the bedroom, and Barb and I held each other for what seemed like forever - after so much separation we were healing; we were being made whole again. We didn't say much; we just held each other and cried, mostly. We had just gone through the hardest experience of our lives, but now we were back together. The stress, the anxiety, the loneliness was slowly going away, but it would take time.

Barb went in and woke Nick up. I remember her walking out with him, holding his hand, saying, "Look who's here." Through sleepy eyes, my now almost 4-year-old son saw me and immediately started crying as he ran across the room in his pajamas with his arms outstretched. I picked him up and sat on the couch holding him for a good half hour, at least. His arms were tightly wrapped around my neck and we both cried. Barb sat next to us crying too.

Barb then woke Adam up and carried him out to the living room where Nick and I were. Nick was standing on the couch next to me with his arm around my neck as Barb tried to give Adam to me. Adam was not having anything to do with me, and he cried in protest when I tried to hold him. Nick kept saying, "It's Daddy, Adam, it's Daddy," but

Adam didn't know who I was. I'm sure he was wondering, who is this guy, and why is he in our house?

It didn't take long for us to melt into a strong family unit. I had about a week to do nothing but be home and spend time with family before we had to move to Fort Hood, Texas, for my next duty assignment in the 6th Air Cavalry. This time, we would be moving as a family.

CHAPTER ELEVEN
The Lone Star State

Before I received orders to go to Korea, I had put in for Helicopter Flight School. After spending so much time in helicopters with the 101st and loving every minute of it, I wanted to be a pilot. I had never flown in an airplane or helicopter until I joined the Army, but I thought that flying was one of the coolest things ever. Most of our training on deployments and in Air Assault School had been done in the "Huey" helicopter, the ones famously used in the Vietnam War. Just before I had enlisted in the spring of 1980, more and more UH-60A Blackhawk helicopters were coming online to replace the old "Hueys." They were beautiful flying machines, and the 101st was getting a lot of them. Not only did I train in them, but I also became friends with some officers who took me up a few times when I was off duty.

I received notification in the mail that I had been accepted. If I still wanted to go, all I had to do was sign some papers, and I would be off to Helicopter Flight School at Fort Rucker, Alabama. The flight school took about a year and I would be promoted to warrant officer upon graduation, which meant a big pay raise, as well as a new job as a pilot. This was good news, and Barb knew how badly I wanted

Loren pilot

to be a pilot. But there was one catch. Upon graduation I had to re-enlist for an additional four years. When I had

Loren realized his dream of being a pilot in the mid 90's

put in the application, I had every intention of making a career in the military; I loved most things about it, and I was good at it. After the tour in Korea, and the year apart from my family, I had a different perspective.

Everyone told me, once you go to Korea you ARE going to go back. It's not a matter of if; it's a matter of when. I talked to Barb about it, and neither of us wanted to go through the hell of being separated for another year again. I told her I would turn down the flight school, and we would get out at the end of my enlistment, which was six short months down the road. Still, I dreamed of becoming a pilot someday.

Texas 1984

Barb's older brother Randy and his wife Dawn were stationed at Fort Hood, and since we only had six months left in the military, they invited us to stay with them and save some money on rent before my enlistment ended.

They had a three-bedroom house and no children yet; so, off to Texas we went. Randy and Dawn were great hosts, and living with them in Texas was a lot of fun. Randy and I spent a lot of time in his garage rebuilding engines and working on cars. I wasn't raised in a mechanic's home; I was raised in a law enforcement officer and builder's home. I could build anything, but I was clueless when it came to mechanics. Randy taught me a lot in those six months, and I enjoyed it. Barb and Dawn were like sisters, and the boys had a great time.

This was 1984. Just a few years earlier, the movie "Urban Cowboy" had come out in theaters and it was a huge hit. Barb and I both loved country music and the movie starring John Travolta, so there was no way we were going to leave Texas without going to Gilley's. Randy and Dawn watched the boys while Barb and I hit the road in search of the mythical movie star bar. Gilley's was in Pasadena, Texas, just outside of Houston, so it's a three-and-a-half-hour drive from Fort Hood.

We arrived well before dark and went inside. We spent a few hours sipping on beer, having dinner, and looking around. The place was big. It had a gift store, a mechanical bull, a rodeo arena, and a HUGE hardwood dance floor out in front of the stage, where a lot of the scenes for the movie were filmed. We sat and talked for a long time, just enjoying each other's company and the bar. To our surprise, Earl Thomas Conley was playing that night. He was well known back then, and had several No. 1 hits on country radio. Barb and I danced the two-step while he played. We tore up the dance floor for hours and probably stayed too late, because by the time we got back home I could hardly keep my eyes open.

In June of 1984 my enlistment ended, and we loaded up the car and headed back to Washington State. This adventure was ending, and we were looking forward to the next, together, as a family.

We had crisscrossed the United States in our travels, but never on a vacation with enough time or money to enjoy the sights. It was always from point A to point B, as quickly as we could. The trip from Texas to Washington was no different. It did, however, take a very long time before we left Texas. For anyone who has traveled there by car you know, the Lone Star State is gigantic!

My dad and I had been talking on the phone (I'm a very forgiving person), and the promise of a good steady job with him led us to Elma, Washington. We rented a duplex on Garden Hill Road and moved in. Work wasn't exactly what I had expected. There was a lot of down time, and we were having a hard time financially. I ended up having to go on food stamps for a few months to help feed the family, something that really bothered me. I had avoided doing that while in the military for four years – just barely.

My brother Wade was working at a rope factory in Anacortes making a decent wage, and when a job opening came available, I applied and got the job. We packed up and moved to Anacortes. My brothers, Kevin and Wade, both lived in Anacortes, along with my mom and her husband, Jim Drovdahl. Mom worked at the Anacortes post office and Jim ran their business, the Shrimp Shack, by the Deception Pass Bridge, just north of Whidbey Island.

Working in a factory was not very satisfying, and I hated being indoors all the time. The owners were very good people to work for, and they treated everyone well, but I could not see myself working in a factory for the rest of my life. Some people can do it and I'm not knocking it. It just wasn't for me. I was working the night shift, taking care of my family with a good wage, but always looking for something else.

Right outside of Anacortes are two oil refineries. Every so often, they shut down for a cleanup, where equipment is taken apart and repaired or cleaned before firing it back up again. Sometimes the shutdowns lasted for a month or more.

The positions at the refineries were really well-paying jobs. I applied and got hired for the next round of shutdowns as a laborer in the pipefitters union. I had tried to get a job running a crane at different places, since that's what I learned in the Army, but most were union jobs that took years waiting on a list to get. I kept my job at the rope factory working nights, and worked the day shift at the refinery.

I had worked there for a couple weeks when I saw some equipment being delivered in the yard just outside of the job shack. My eyes got big as I saw them unloading a small deck crane. I had no idea how a person would get the job to run that small crane, but I was determined to do everything I could to be the one. At the very least, I wasn't going to be shy about letting the powers that be know I could do it.

Our foreman was a large man who didn't talk much to lowly laborers like myself, at least I hadn't seen him do it. When he spoke you would have thought that God himself was talking, because people moved and said "Yes sir" a lot. I had never talked to him, nor he to me, but I knew if someone was going to put me in the operator's seat of that crane it was going to be him. I was going to make a point of being in the right place at the right time when he showed up for work on the next shift. I knew there was a small window of opportunity to make my case before he disappeared into the job shack, only to be seen occasionally during the shift. I'm sure he was inside going over blueprints, order forms, and crew lists all the time as he directed the supervisors under him, and managed hundreds of workers just like me.

Having just spent the last four years in the military, I understood the chain of command. You don't just walk into the commander's office and start at the top of the food chain. I had a conversation with my direct supervisor about running the crane, but he didn't seem interested in taking it anywhere. He said that they probably already had an operator or the crane wouldn't be here. That was the end of that, as far as he was concerned, but not for me.

The next day I showed up just a little bit early. I grabbed a piece of pipe, so it looked like I was doing something constructive as I walked back and forth passing the job shack. I kept my eye on the parking lot entrance for the boss, and soon, he came walking across the parking lot as his next-in-line supervisors started to gather and walk with him. I assumed they were talking about the crane operator job.

I timed it just right as he walked around the corner of the job shack with the other supervisors in tow, and we met right at the corner just before he went up the stairs to his office. He and the crowd around him stopped with me right in front of them, still holding the pipe. He looked a little startled and a bit annoyed, but I quickly blurted out: "Sir, I'm Loren Culp, a U.S. Army veteran; I was the honor graduate of the Army Crane Operator School at Fort Leonard Wood, Missouri. I can run that carry deck crane. If you would give me the chance, I won't let you down." He looked me up and down, and without saying a word to me, he looked at one of his supervisors and told him to have someone test me on the crane. Then he walked around me and into his office. I never talked to him again.

Later that day, my immediate supervisor sent me to his supervisor. He told me that it looked like I would be tested on the crane. I was elated. I found the supervisor and he told me, "Go get warmed up on that crane," and I did. I ran over to it, checked the oil, fuel and tires, and then fired it up. This was huge! I was very nervous and excited. If I passed this test, I would be an operator. Not only would it get me out of the muck and mess that a laborer often finds himself in, but it meant a substantial raise in my hourly wage.

This carry deck crane was much smaller than what I had operated in the Army. It was about the size of a pickup truck. I had been on cranes in the Army that would lift 40 to 60 tons and reach many stories up in the air, so although I knew how to operate cranes, I had never been on THIS type of crane. My anxiety level was high.

Generally, every crane – no matter what the size is – does the same job. It picks stuff up and moves it. The controls on most heavy equipment vary from one manufacturer to another, so I spent about 30 minutes becoming familiar with this one. I saw the foreman waving me over from across the yard; they were ready, but was I? I put it in gear and pushed the gas pedal. The engine revved, but the crane didn't move! Oh crap, what's wrong? I started to panic and then I saw it – the parking brake. I pulled the brake off and I drove the crane over to him. I was praying the whole way, trying to calm myself. I thanked God for the opportunity and asked Him to please help me do a good job. As usual, I felt that God was with me.

With a couple of laborers to do the rigging, he had me unload and then load a few items onto the back of a flatbed truck, and then move them around the yard. Success! He came over to the window of the crane and told me I had the job, and then introduced me to my new supervisor. I ran the crane the rest of the time on that shutdown and continued to work at the rope factory at the same time. Working two jobs, as anyone who has done it can tell you, isn't easy – but sometimes, it's necessary to get ahead. This one little opportunity led to other jobs, running even bigger cranes in three different refineries, and helped my family financially.

Lesson learned: never be afraid to reach for the brass ring – or the parking brake.

Running My Own Show

My older brother Randy Culp was running his own construction business in the Olympia area, and he had a position on his framing crew open up. My love for building and working outdoors was always nagging at me while I worked in the rope factory, so when he offered me a job with his company, I jumped at the chance and we moved from Anacortes to Thurston County. We rented a place on 5 acres right outside of the small town of Rainier, and I went to work. Little did I know at the time, but this decision would change the trajectory of my life and career for decades to come. The foreman on the crew was Paul Thornock. Paul was and is a very focused man, and a great teacher. He knows his craft inside and out. I was like a sponge absorbing knowledge from him and the No. 2 person on the crew, Mark Trehune.

I had helped build houses in the past working with my dad, but the system that Paul taught me was absolutely the best, most efficient way to frame a house that I had ever seen. To this day, I have never seen anything better. Along with working full time, I would pick up work on the side as well – small patios, wood decks, and things like that. I worked on those projects after work and on the weekends, and Paul would come and help me sometimes.

Paul was a great teacher. I remember him saying many times, "I'm only going to show you this once, so pay attention." I did pay attention, and after working under him for a couple of years, I started my own construction business in 1988. The opportunity that Randy gave me to work for him changed things in my life for decades, and I will always be thankful to him, Paul, and Mark.

The late '80s was the beginning of a housing boom that lasted for many years. It seemed everyone was building or buying a house, and the market was hot. Starting your own business from scratch is an expensive endeavor, but one I yearned for. I needed a lot of tools and equipment. I would need air compressors, nail guns, a generator, and a chainsaw. For the concrete foundation work I was going to start doing, I would also need concrete forms or panels. I used 2-foot-by-8-foot, $1\frac{1}{8}$-inch-thick plywood concrete panels for forms. These were not cheap, nor were they light. I had work lined up, but I needed thousands of dollars for forms and a way to haul them. Where there's a will, there's a way.

CHAPTER TWELVE

I contacted the owner of Tanglewilde Lumber, Mr. Detlef-sen, in Lacey where I had been getting supplies for years. I talked to him about my new business venture, and told him of the work I had lined up. He extended me credit on the concrete forms that I needed by giving me a few months to pay them off. At the time, I had only an old, small Datsun pickup truck that I had bought from my Grandpa Culp for $600 on monthly payments. I found a homemade single axle trailer and bought that to tow behind the pickup. I hauled about 10 panels in the truck and 20 or so in the trailer. Both were overloaded and I'm sure way past the weight limit, but I drove slowly, moving panels from one job site to another, and made do with multiple trips. I only had one employee at the time, but starting in 1988 at the ripe old age of 27, I was in business for myself doing foundations, some framing, and flatwork here and there.

I quickly added to my crew, rounding it out at three people most of the time and expanding it to nearly 20 on bigger jobs. With my training from Paul, Randy, and Mark, I soon had a crew that knew what they were doing. We would roll onto a job site in the morning, set up the forms for the footing, and pour concrete with an accel-erant in it at about 10 a.m. We'd have lunch, and then set up the wall panels and pour the walls by 2 p.m. We would start stripping forms that same day, ready for the next. It was grueling, fast-paced, dirty work, but there is nothing wrong with a dirty job – it builds character. I soon had a full-size pickup with a custom trailer that would haul all of my forms in one trip.

I went through some employees; hard work isn't for everyone, especially at the pace I worked. After a couple of years, doing mainly foundations with some framing and concrete flatwork, I moved into more concrete flatwork, driveways, garage floors, sidewalks, and patios. The income was better, and packing panels is backbreaking work. I wasn't getting any younger.

A lean mean framing machine

Building a Home With No Money

After building many homes for other people, Barb and I wanted to build our own, so I went to our bank and applied for a loan. We had good credit and we thought that there shouldn't be any problem. I was wrong. After submitting our loan application, I had a meeting with the manager. He told me that everything looked good, except that I had only been in business for myself for a couple years. They were worried that something could happen and that I might go out of business before the house was completed. They wanted to see me in business for a longer period of time, maybe a year more.

That was not how I saw things, and that was definitely not the answer I was looking for. Business was great, jobs were coming in, and we were saving money – but that is not how they saw it. Many businesses fail in the first few years, and they were not willing to take the risk of having a half-built house on their hands because of the inexperience of a 29-year-old.

The banker told me that if I wanted to buy an existing house, they would approve that loan, because it was less risky for them. Buying an already built house and building a home are two completely different animals. As a builder, I didn't want to pay a high price for a house that I could build myself and have immediate equity. I asked the banker, "If this house was already built, then would you loan us the money?" He said yes. I told him to be ready, because the house would be done within 90 days, and we would need to close on the loan quickly.

I left that meeting knowing that I could do it, but not knowing if all the pieces would fall into place so I could get started. I already had the blueprints for an 1800-square-foot, three-bedroom home and an earnest money down on 3 acres, just outside of Olympia on Steamboat Island Road.

I contacted all of the subcontractors and suppliers that I had come to know and work with. I told all of them about the situation, and asked if they would be willing to wait up to 60 to 90 days for payment on the work or materials they would provide for the house. All of them said yes. I talked to a former customer of mine who I knew had a little money to invest, and he agreed to buy the land

and hold a contract with me until the bank financing was done. Then, I went to work.

I set up a tight work schedule and called all the subcontractors and told them the schedule. I needed everyone to execute flawlessly and to be on time, no matter what. We excavated for the foundation that next week, and within a couple days, the foundation was finished and we had the floor framed and sheeted. The well driller was coming in a couple days, and I had to decide where to drill the well. I researched and saw that the properties around us had very deep wells, like 150 to 200 feet deep. To drill that deep would be a huge expense that would strain our budget.

One evening just before dark, I walked the property and prayed for God to help me find a spot with water. We could not afford a dry well nor a deep one. As I was walking the property, praying, I felt a strong tingle like the hair was standing up on the back of my head. I put a stake in the ground where I stood, and that's where the well was dug a few days later. They hit good, clean, plentiful water at about 65 feet down. I was very happy and thankful.

A week later, we had the entire house framed. My good friend, Ron Springer, who still owns Springer Plumbing with his wife Diane, was putting the plumbing in while the roofing was going on. It all went like clockwork. After the plumbing was roughed in, the electricians and heating contractors came in. Then it was insulation, sheetrock, and paint. The painting was done by another really good friend of mine, Walt Johnson, who still owns W.E. Davis painting company in Tumwater. I put in the kitchen and bathroom cabinets, hung the doors, and installed the trim. The floor covering company came in and did the carpet, tile, and countertops.

Other than a few minor things still to be done, like closet shelves and a mailbox, we were ready to move in after only 57 days. It was exhausting. After our house's foundation and framing were completed, I still had to do customer work to maintain an income. There were many late nights, but it was well worth it.

I went to the bank with pictures of the house, and they started to work on closing and the scheduling of their inspectors. The banker was amazed at what we had accomplished, and within a few weeks, the loan closed and everyone was paid. We moved out of the place in Rainier to our first new home. After word got around to the other bankers in the area, I never had a problem borrowing money from a bank, until the financial crisis many years later.

I learned very quickly about the pitfalls of owning and running your own construction business, especially as a subcontractor. There are a lot of good, honest contractors like Todd Hanson, who I did work for for years. He always paid on time, and I knew I could count on him. My son Adam, whom I later sold my business to, still does work for Todd to this day. I also learned the hard way that there are a lot of dishonest contractors, and a couple of them got me in trouble with the tax man.

In all my years as a contractor, I never had a problem with a customer concerning the quality of my work. I all too often had a problem getting paid, though. In the concrete business, summertime is slam time; you do as many jobs as you can get your hands on. In the winter, it's hit or miss, because you can't pour a driveway in the rain and turn out a good product. In the wintertime, finances can get tight in western Washington, because it rains more than it doesn't. If a contractor is slow to pay or doesn't pay at all, it can sink a small contractor. I've spent my fair share of time on the front porch of a contractor's house demanding to get paid, only to be told, "I'll have the money next week." Sometimes "next week" never came, and I had a few contractors that just "disappeared." In the early '90s I hit a rough patch, and I found out the hard way that the State doesn't mess around. I got behind on taxes and was working as hard as I could to catch up.

Apparently, it wasn't quickly enough. One day, I got a call from my bank: there were insufficient funds to cover checks that were coming in, and it was because the State had cleared out my account. There was no hearing, there was no court date – they just took it. It was right after the first of the month when most contractors paid me, and I had just paid all of my suppliers by check – and now the checks were bouncing. I ended up getting everyone paid, including the State, but I learned a valuable lesson as a young business owner.

The government isn't interested in your success or putting food on your table or paying your suppliers. The State is interested in the State, period. No excuses, no delays. If you don't pay when they say, it could ruin you. That experience made me realize that I was not just in business with myself – I had a partner, the government, and they have no soul. Lesson learned, my fault, thank you sir, may I have another? Wouldn't it be great if we had a government that cared and showed a little bit of heart for hard-working citizens and small business owners, like it does for those who choose not to work?

Hunting

One thing that has remained consistent in my life is my love for hunting. From age 8 when I shot my first deer on Marrowstone Island, I have always loved hunting. I love the challenge of sneaking through the woods trying to find a deer or elk. One-on-one with a wild animal . . . nothing compares. Bringing home good, clean, healthy meat for the dinner table is the best way to ensure that you know where your food comes from. Spending time with family around the campfire at "camp" is something that I have missed over the last few years because of work and the campaign.

We raised our boys in the woods. Almost every weekend for 10 years starting in the late '80s, we hunted with our hounds. When it was legal and the boys were young, we hunted with dogs for raccoons, bobcats, cougars, and bears. When I was a young boy, we had hounds, and hunted with them just like my Grandpa Culp did with my dad. There is nothing like the *mountain music* ringing up from a canyon when the dogs are on the hot track of an animal. As I said in my previous book *American Cop*, if you have never experienced hunting with dogs, you need to read the book or watch the movie *Where the Red Fern Grows*. The bond shared between dogs and humans is a strong one, whether they are hunting dogs or house dogs, but having that bond with a pack of hounds who love to hunt is something very special.

Running around the woods in the mountains with family is a much better place for kids to grow up than in front of the TV or a video game. The experiences we've had up close and personal with wild animals isn't something you can do in front of a TV. And the great thing about hunting with hounds is, you don't have to kill anything to have a successful hunt. Cats and bears climb up trees to get away from dogs, and most of our adventures into the mountains with hounds ended up with pictures or videos and the animal going free.

We had many adventures in the Olympic Mountains as a family with our dogs. Sometimes, it was a weekend camping trip; other times, it was a day trip up to Spider Lake, just outside of Shelton. Having memories of hunting with dogs as a boy, I knew I wanted to share that with my boys, so I set out to make it happen.

In the late '80s, I got a young hound that someone was giving away, and we started hunting bobcats. Well, let me rephrase that. We started trying to hunt for bobcats. I only had a dozen problems with my new hound recruit. The biggest one was, I didn't have any other hounds, especially an experienced one, to teach the young one. Looks don't make a successful hunting dog, and the best way to train them is to have an older experienced dog to lead them. An experienced dog will keep a younger one from running coyotes or deer, which can be very frustrating. By chance (or was it?), I ran across a man in the woods one day who completely changed our hound hunting life, and we are friends to this day. His name is John Fuller. To those who know him, his nickname is Long John. John is well over 6 feet tall; I've never asked him, but I'm assuming that's why he got the nickname.

After getting the free hound, Nick, Adam, and I headed for the woods after a fresh snow to try and find a cat track. We still lived in Rainier at the time and we made our way into the Vail Tree Farm. Vail is a vast chunk of land, about 250 square miles, owned by the Weyerhaeuser Timber company. Back then, the gates were open and hunting was allowed. We were driving around in the snow looking for bobcat tracks. After an hour or so without seeing anything, we came around the corner and saw a couple of other trucks parking on the side of the road. That's the first time I ever saw Long John. Little did either of us know at the time, but it would lead to he and I being hunting partners and lifelong friends. He had treed a bobcat just off the road, and I asked if the boys and I could go into the tree with him. He told us to come on, and we did. Sure enough, his dogs and his friend's dogs had a bobcat up the tree.

The boys loved their dogs

Bobcat

Hunting dogs

During hunting season, we spent almost every weekend of the next decade as hunting partners. He was and is like an uncle to my boys, and like a brother to me.

We put many bobcats and cougars up a tree with our hunting dogs, and many times I would climb up in the tree with them to get close-up pictures and video.

Cougar

Bobcats and cougars were plentiful before they outlawed hunting them with dogs, and they are extremely overpopulated now that dogs have been outlawed. We have treed as many as five cougars at the same time in two different trees. We also hunted elk and deer together with bows and arrows. I could write a book much larger than this one with the stories of every hunt we had.

Long John

I'll end this chapter with this: The citizens of Washington State screwed up big time by letting the Humane Society of the United States convince them that hound hunting needed to be eliminated. They are not your local humane society;

Adam pumping concrete

they don't have animal shelters. They are a rabid far-left organization that's hell-bent on ending the use of animals across the board, even as pets. They spent millions on advertising and propaganda to end it here in Washington, and it's a travesty. Cougars are very overpopulated and they eat a lot of deer and elk. Nuff said?

When our family wasn't hunting with the dogs or hunting for deer and elk, we spent a lot of time riding dirt bikes and camping. Just like when I was growing up, our boys learned how to work hard from an early age. They came with me many times on jobs, and both were employed in the family business for some time. They have both grown into a couple of good men, and our family has grown to include eight grandchildren.

Nick and Adam helping their dad build a fence

Decorative Concrete

CHAPTER FIFTEEN

My "Empire" Crumbles

Barb and I took full advantage of the tax laws regarding the sale of our home. After two years we would sell and rebuild, and invest the profit into the next house, with no income taxes due on the sale. Those were the rules. After we did about five homes this way, we started looking for and investing in rental property.

I would go on the county website, find land in rural areas that was zoned multi-family, and then drive around looking at the properties. The first deal I made was on one of these drives, and it resulted in us building our first two duplexes in the Rochester area.

The initial contract was a handwritten one made with a farmer behind Johnny's Auction House in Grand Mound. I had seen the 2-acre piece of land on a website, and I drove to it. It was a flat field with good access, so I went next door to the owner's house and asked him if he was interested in selling that piece of land. Within a half hour, we negotiated a fair price and I wrote out a basic earnest money agreement on a notepad, which I took to the title company. Within a few months, we had our first rental units up and rented. We duplicated this process many times. I was an avid reader of the *Rich Dad Poor Dad* books written by Robert Kiyosaki and I liked his take on investments. If you haven't ever read his books, I highly recommend them. I also highly recommend getting his financial education board game, Cashflow. It's fun for the whole family, and even teens can learn a lot about money and investing by playing that game.

After finishing those two duplexes, we built another one in Rochester. Then we sold those three and built nine more. If I had a crystal ball, I might have stopped then, but I didn't have one and don't believe in them anyway. My brother Randy and I went in as partners on a large development.

Then came the financial crisis of the mid-to-late 2000s. The crisis ended up pretty much wiping Barb and me out. All of a sudden, banks weren't loaning money, and potential renters were either staying home with mom and dad, or moving back home to save money. The rental market and real estate in general crashed. I foolishly believed President Bush when he said relief was coming; remember HARP and TARP?

CHAPTER FIFTEEN

Americans were being lied to on a grand scale. There never was any help with refinancing for us "little people." The only people who got any help were the big banks. They got bailed out in a huge way at the expense of taxpayers. We held on as long as we could, which was a long time. We used up all of our savings, making payments and paying taxes on mostly empty units. I tried to refinance with the banks that held the mortgages, but they weren't loaning; they were waiting on their bailout. We got a few of the duplexes sold at fire sale prices, but the rest went back to the bank. Well, that was fun – 20 years of working hard and investing for my family's future, down the drain.

That whole "financial crisis" left a bad taste in my mouth, to say the least. The biggest problem I have with the whole thing is that it's not a level playing field. If you are politically connected and have "friends" in the right places, you become "too big to fail" and get rewarded, no matter what. There were many people much bigger than us who lost everything. I was thankful to walk away without having to declare bankruptcy, but I'd had enough of the building game and was not inclined to start from scratch in that field. I decided to realize my childhood dream; that opportunity was right around the corner. I look back on the financial crisis now not as a curse or a failure; I look back on it as a blessing and a learning experience. Had it not been for the financial crisis, I would have never realized my dream or received the blessings that came with it. I would have never been in the position to stand up for citizens' rights. I would have never written *American Cop*, and I would have never run for political office. I would have never met most of you reading this right now. It's funny how things work out; even things we think are not good can turn out to be a blessing.

Since we are on the subject of things not working out as we sometimes plan, I'm going to talk a little bit about motivation and having a positive mental attitude, and how I've made it through rough patches in my life. Hopefully, it will help you out as well. So many times in our lives, it would be really easy to give up, to give in, to raise the white flag of surrender and remove ourselves from the "battlefield" of life. But think about this:

What motivates you? Have you thought about that lately? In today's world, it's easy to lose your motivation with all the negative news, negative outcomes in life or in politics, and just negative people in general. I don't have time for negativity; I always strive to be motivated, no matter what's going on.

What motivates you in your day-to-day life may not be the same thing that motivates your friends, co-workers, or family. Each of us has something we are born with that moves us to focus on success, but it's easily stifled if we don't exercise it or have the right mindset. We don't always achieve our idea of success, but most people always strive to win in one form or another. Whether it's trying to earn good grades in school, competing to sell Girl Scout cookies (which I never did, by the way), competing in sports, competing against other people in an attempt to get a better job, or competing in the business world, we all pretty much aim to succeed.

I remember when I first started my own business in 1988. My Grandpa told me, "Always give your customer more than they expect." Before that, he told me, "Always give your boss more than they deserve." Always going the extra mile, showing up early or staying late, always working harder than is needed, expecting nothing in return – that builds character. Knowing you did your best builds confidence, but it all stems from motivation, and what motivates you.

We don't always have control over the situations we are put into in life; in fact, I would say that there are many situations in life that we do not have control over. One example of this is when we were born. Right from the first day of our lives, we have zero control over the family we are born into or where we are born. I highly doubt that before our birth, we had a menu of options to choose from. Can you imagine scrolling through that menu? "No, they don't have a Corvette; No, they live in a single-wide; Nope, they don't have any money . . . OK there, that looks like a good family, I'll take that one." I doubt we have that option; if we did, who would choose to be born into poverty or drug addiction or alcoholism or abuse? All of those things can be overcome, and I've seen many people overcome them, but those choices probably wouldn't be at the top of anyone's list!

So, being born is the first situation in life that we are all forced into. Sometimes it's good and sometimes it's bad, but we had no control. We are all forced into situations that we have no control over, but what we have to remember is: no matter how bad things may seem in the moment, we all have inside of us the drive, the motivation, and the will to succeed – we are born with it.

Remembering that you can't always have total control over your life – or a particular situation – helps when your plans don't work out how you planned. What motivated us to take our first breath upon entering this world is still inside each one of us. Some people have suppressed it after a life of struggle. How many times can you be beat down and keep going?

I say, every time! I wake up every day excited to make that day the best I can. What challenges will I face today, who can I help today, what can I do to make this a better place? No matter what, I always try to do my best, and it doesn't start when I open my eyes in the morning. It starts before I close my eyes the night before.

Before I go to sleep every night, I say a prayer. I thank God for the day I had, and the lessons I learned. Even if it was a bad day, it doesn't matter; and then as I drift off to sleep, in my head, I repeat over and over, "Tomorrow is going to be a good day, because God is in charge," and it works. Installing the correct mindset at night ensures you are programmed for success the next day. Having faith and knowing that God is in charge, no matter what, is a comforting feeling. When I do my best, whether most people would call what I did a success or not, I'm comforted by knowing I succeeded in trying my best at the time. If I feel like I could've done better, if maybe I missed the mark somehow . . . well, that's what tomorrow is for.

That's what motivates me and that's how I stay motivated. My hope for all of us is that we take each day and look at it as a building block. Day after day, adding another block to our lives. We have to work to keep alive in our hearts and minds, what we were born with – and that's the never-ending yearning to succeed, even if it's only to take the very next breath. If you've lost a little bit of that through the years, you can get it back – one day at a time, one thought at a time, one breath at a time. We all need that warrior mentality. It just takes a positive mental attitude and a little bit of prayer.

CHAPTER SIXTEEN

There's a New Cop in Town

When one door shuts, God opens another, always. No matter how devastating something feels, there is always hope when you know you are not the one in charge of things that happen in this world. All a person can do is their best and never give up. When you fall flat on your face, as far as I'm concerned, there isn't anything else to do but get back up, thank God for the opportunity, dust yourself off, and continue driving on.

That's the warrior mentality. That's the difference between winners and losers. To me, it's common sense. "Defeat" are the two things with 10 toes connected to your legs that you put into your work boots every day and continue to march forward. I've always had faith. I was raised in a Christian home and we raised our boys that way. I believe that God has a plan for each of us. Sometimes it does not include what we think or plan, but that's OK. I'm good with that; I am His servant and no matter what happens, I have faith that God will provide, as long as I continue to give it my best. Things work out on His timeline and according to His will.

I have witnessed things in my life that have no rational explanation. I've already mentioned the well we dug for our first home. That same thing happened again on the property we live on now in Republic. Our neighboring properties have very deep wells. One of the wells is over 300 feet deep, producing only a few gallons of water per minute. I walked around our property just like the first time, and prayed. I experienced the same *hair on the back of my neck standing up feeling*, and put a stake in the ground. The well driller showed up the next day and hit over 20 gallons per minute at 50 feet down. Miracle? Coincidence? I believe it was an answered prayer.

When I was about 12 years old, I saw a young man, about 20 years old, lift a full-size overturned farm tractor up by the back wheel to save my brother, who was trapped under it. We lived on the farm on Marrowstone Island at the time, and someone, I can't remember who, got my mom's car stuck in the mud in one of our fields. My older brother Randy hooked a chain to the front of the car axle and to the back of our old tractor. He told me to put the car in drive when he said "go," so he could pull it out with the tractor. I could barely see over the steering wheel, but I was ready. Kevin and Wade were in the front seat with me. In the headlights of the car, I saw Randy get on the tractor and put it in gear. When the chain came tight, the front of the tractor came up and it flipped over backwards right in front of the car, pinning Randy underneath it. I never heard him say "go" and it happened fast. I jumped out of the car into the headlights as the engine on the tractor shut off. I was thinking that my brother was dead.

Thankfully he wasn't dead, but he was pinned to the ground by the steering wheel of the overturned tractor on his leg. He moaned, "Get help!" Kevin ran to the Johnsons's house across the road for help because Dad wasn't home. I could do nothing but talk to Randy, and apologize for not hearing him say "go." He was conscious, but in a tremendous amount of pain.

Mark Johnson came running across the field out of the darkness with Kevin not far behind. He took a look at the situation, and told us to get ready to help pull Randy out. He grabbed the large back tire of the tractor and lifted. All by himself, he lifted that tractor tire up high enough for us to help Randy slide out from under the steering wheel. Once we had him clear, the tractor slammed back down.

Was that a miracle? I think so. We went back the next day, and Mark could not lift the tractor tire, no matter how hard he tried. He couldn't even get the tractor to move at all. Was it pure adrenaline? I'm sure that helped, but that wasn't all that was in play that night, it was a big tractor after all. God always provides.

Barb and I had bought 40 acres just outside of Republic that we had planned on retiring to when the time came. We built a shop with a small apartment right in the middle of our 40 acres. It is a beautiful piece of land, with a couple of benches and rolling meadows. It's at the end of a private driveway, a half-mile from the gravel county road. On the back side of our property is a couple hundred acres of state land, so we don't have to worry about neighbors. We have plenty of elbow room and we've got a beautiful view of Gibraltar Mountain and the valley below.

There is lots of wildlife that call our area home, and we have seen bobcats, whitetail and mule deer, moose, and a few black bears on our property. Friends and family have put meat in the freezer by hunting on our property; it's not uncommon in the evening to see a couple dozen deer grazing in our fields. We love it here; it is our piece of heaven on earth.

It was one day while we were enjoying the peace and quiet of another day here that I saw the ad in the local paper for a police officer position in Republic. Having been raised in a law enforcement household, it was my dream as a child to be a police officer. I spent a lot of time with my dad and his friends, who were also in law enforcement at the time. I had a lot of respect for deputies and police. Life had taken me in a different direction up until this point, and now a door was opening for another adventure.

CHAPTER SIXTEEN

Barb thought I was a little bit crazy to apply for a police job at 49 years old and I couldn't disagree with her, but I knew if I didn't do it then, I would be too old really soon – if I wasn't already. We wanted to stay in Republic but I wasn't interested in going back into the building game, even though there was plenty of that type of work available.

I applied for the police job and got hired by the chief at the time, Brett Roberts. A permanent job was contingent on me passing the police academy. I knew it was going to be hard at my age. Most people who apply for law enforcement jobs are young, usually in their 20s or 30s, and that is what the police academy is geared for. It's not a retirement home training program.

When I showed up in Burien for the PAT (Physical Ability Test), I had already been working out at home. I could knock out the push-ups and sit-ups because I had spent years finishing concrete and pounding nails. The timed run is what worried me. Running was easy in basic training in the Army, but I was 19 years old then. Here I was 30 years older, ready to give it a go with old joints and bones that didn't function quite like they did in my prime. My chief was there to observe the tests, and I meant to give it my best. The staff of the academy were there, trying their best to resemble drill sergeants with new recruits. *Been there, done that,* I thought to myself as I prepared for the run.

I thought, *All I have to do is get my overweight, old carcass across the finish line with time to spare* – and I didn't care if it was by just one second, as long as it was under the allotted time. Off I went at a steady pace around the track. I knew I had to push myself into the not-so-comfort zone and make it happen. Thoughts of when I was young and hunting elk with my dad went through my mind. When we would get on a herd of elk, his method of hunting was to stay on them and move as fast as he could, hoping to get a shot at one when the herd stopped to look back at what was chasing them. It was effective many times.

I remember at 12 years old, when I shot my first elk, trying to keep up with him going through the woods. He would stop and wait for me sometimes, and I remember telling him, "I can't breathe." He would tell me, "Keep going, you'll get your second wind soon enough," and off he would go. Eventually I learned what he meant, because it did happen.

This run in the PAT test at 49 years old was a struggle. I kept thinking, *Where is my second wind? Maybe I lost it, maybe at 49 it isn't there anymore.* After a few laps around the track, I was sucking wind really badly and felt like I was going to die . . . or at least pass out. I slowed to a fast walk, trying to catch my breath, but it wasn't working. Then the thoughts in my head came. *What are you doing!!?* I remembered basic training and elk hunting all at the same time.

CHAPTER SIXTEEN

This was my shot! In less than 10 minutes, this would be over, one way or another. This was no time to slack off – if I die, I die. I began to run, and sure enough, I caught my second wind and began to pass people. When I came around the last corner on the track, there were several people 20 years my junior behind me, and I was pushing myself as hard as I could. Warrior mentality, Bravo Bulls, Air Assault, a yellow bird . . . all those things were coming out as I went to a full-out sprint on the last straight stretch. I did it with plenty of time left. My legs were like rubber, but I made it!

The almost six months in the academy were not at all like basic training and AIT in the Army. It was more a mixture of college law classes, wrestling practice, getting your ass kicked in fighting scenarios, and basic training in the Army all mixed together.

I was almost let go from the academy for an injury. One morning, we were practicing drills in the parking lot and then running to the next station. I severely pulled a calf muscle during one of the runs. No matter what I tried to do to stretch it out, I was limping badly. I did my best to not let it show, but a couple of days later during PT in the gym, one of the instructors saw me limping while we were running. I was pulled aside and "addressed" up one side and down the other for not reporting an injury. I was examined, and I pleaded with the instructor to please not send me home. "This is my one shot; I can do it!" I said. I don't know why, but he let me stay once I was cleared by a doctor (with whom I also pleaded). I was limping around for a couple of weeks, but my leg got a little bit better. Even though I still had a slight limp at graduation, I made it. I had become a state certified Peace Officer.

Chief Roberts was gone when I returned to Republic from the Academy. His brother had been severely wounded in the military, so he had retired from police work to help his brother. I never had a chance to work with him in Republic, but I will be forever grateful for him taking a chance on an "old man." It led to almost 11 years of serving my hometown. I brought the same work ethic I had learned and used during my previous careers to law enforcement. My grandfather had told me years earlier, when I started my own business, "Always give the customer, your boss, more than they expect." I know that most citizens in Republic would tell you to this very day that I did just that.

They helped me raise the funds through donations to get the city's first narcotics K9. Businesses, citizens, and our local Eagles helped out in a big way. There was a HUGE drug problem in Republic and in the surrounding Ferry County when I first started work here. I recognized it, as most police officers and citizens do, as the root cause of most of the crime. The thefts, the assaults, burglaries, and domestic violence almost always resulted from the root cause, addiction.

My first K9 was Isko, a beautiful, all-black German Shepherd who was donated to us by a Snohomish officer, Suzanne Eviston. Isko was 3 years old when I got him, and as a result of donations, we went to the State Narcotics K9 Academy in Shelton. After graduation, we went to work. K9 Isko was a dream to work with, and we began to make a dent in the crimes in Republic. He was also great in the local schools. We did many demonstrations for the students and they loved him.

I worked with several members of the narcotics task force, but there are a couple of detectives in particular who I want to mention: Deputy Talon Venturo with the Ferry County Sheriff's Office and Jodie Barcus from the Colville Tribal Police. Both were members of the North Central Washington Narcotics Task Force at the time, and both had done many narcotics cases. They, along with a few others, received the key to the City of Republic. With their help in coaching and training me, we took down many dealers. There were many nights spent in

Detective's Jodie Barcus and Talon Venturo receive the Key to the City of Republic

undercover vehicles in Republic, working informants and doing supervised buys from several dealers right in town. We did the same with several dealers out in the county, as well. I would say that Republic was overrun with heroin and meth at the time, so it was a target-rich environment, to say the least.

I soon became very efficient at writing search warrants and doing narcotics cases. The first big pushback against the dealers was a multiple resident bust that we did with other members from the task force. After completing multiple buys of heroin and meth over a long period of time and building an airtight case, we executed the warrants at the same time on all three residences. It resulted in a large amount of heroin and meth being seized as evidence, and about 12 people being arrested and put in jail, with some going to prison. But that was just the tip of the iceberg. In a one-year period we did about 70 cases in and around Republic, when prior to that there had only been a handful. I learned really quickly about the human toll of the drug trade – the ruined lives, the hopelessness, and the loss of life caused by being stuck in the cycle of addiction.

I went into too many homes and did far too many death investigations, with many of them involving a needle in the arm of the deceased. Most were young people, in what should have been the prime of their lives. Some couldn't deal with the addiction and the suffering that came with it. They ended their lives with a rope around their neck or died from overdoses. To see the death and destruction of so many individuals and families was hard. I made it my goal to help as many as I could.

I am very proud to say that we helped many with strict enforcement of the laws, coupled with compassionate treatment. I now consider many who were arrested to be friends, and I see them all the time in Republic and the surrounding area. Some are now business owners, and all are good

K9 Isko

people living a clean life. Many of them are raising families here. I'm very proud of them and happy I could play a small part in what helped them onto the right track. The Mayor awarded me the Key to the City and soon promoted me to chief of police.

Sadly, K9 Isko died in my arms at the Ferry County Hospital Emergency Room one night in January a few years ago, but not before leaving

K9 Isko (Photo Courtsey of Chris Thew)

his mark on this community. A tumor that we didn't know about burst inside him and he bled to death very quickly. As I held him in my arms, I watched the life leave his eyes as I cried like a helpless baby. He was my partner, my buddy, and my friend.

The community came together to honor K9 Isko in a large memorial at the school. The place was packed as people spoke about him and how he helped our town. One in particular was John Donner, a young man who many of you have come to know through my campaign for governor. John was helped by Isko's great nose and is one of the many who has chosen to live a good life since. John thanked Isko for helping him, and it was all that I could do, throughout the service and John's words, to keep from crying in public. The Okanogan County Sheriff's Office honor guard came and helped us with the flag ceremony as Isko was honored with a flag draped coffin. Before and after the service at the school, law enforcement, fire, and ambulance crews from all over the area came to honor the service of my partner with a funeral procession through the city.

Citizens lined the street as the emergency vehicles slowly drove through town with their red and blue lights on, escorting Isko in his coffin, in my truck. When dispatch did a final call for K9 Isko over the radio, I wasn't the only officer who couldn't hold back the tears. K9 Isko's final resting place is just outside my house here in Republic. He will always have a place in my heart, and in so many others hearts as well. He had a large impact on a small town, to say the least.

After Isko passed, word spread around the country and with the help of rock legend Ted Nugent, I soon had a new K9. The owners of Phoenix Protective Corp. in Spokane, JC and Sheila, donated K9 Karma to me. They paid for a two-week training trip for me to meet Karma in California so I could get to know him and train with him. K9 Karma was a rescue dog; he was found at a high-kill shelter in California, removed, and put through training. He was not only a narcotics detection dog; he was also trained in patrol work. We were soon on a trip in my patrol vehicle heading back to Washington State, where we were certified in narcotics work together.

Our first night back in Republic, we were called out by Ferry County to assist in a traffic stop. K9 Karma quickly started making a name for himself, because he detected meth in not just one, but two, vehicles that night. We soon went through the 10-week patrol dog school with the Spokane Police Department, and returned to Republic as a dual-purpose K9 team. Karma not only helped with narcotics detection, but he also helped in locating dangerous felons hiding in the woods and in searching buildings while officers stayed safely outside.

One memorable case happened about a year after we got back from the patrol academy. A very bad man had beat up his girlfriend in a remote cabin in the hills of Ferry County. The deputies had dispatched to call us to come out, and we responded to the scene. It was about 2:00 a.m. and the deputies told me that it was a felony assault; the suspect had left the cabin armed with a knife about two hours prior. There was no known direction of travel, so I took K9 Karma out of my car and put him in a harness with a long line attached. I gave him the command to search for a person and we began to circle the cabin.

During training, K9 Karma had tracked and located a person who had walked through the woods four hours earlier, so I was confident that we were going to find the track and the person. However, there are many factors that come into play. It was a very dry and warm night, with a little moonlight. We circled about halfway around the cabin and Karma started pulling on his long line, heading up the hill away from the cabin. I had two deputies close to me

K9 Karma

as we followed Karma up the hill, through the trees and low brush. We went uphill for about 100 yards, and then he made a small circle until he found the track again. He led us for about 50 yards, and then stopped and sat down, looking back at me with just his head above the low bushes.

K9 Karma – Photo courtesy of the best 911 dispatcher ever, Carmita Barnes

During training, he was taught that if he comes across
any item that has the scent of the person we are tracking

that he should sit (and that he'll receive a reward). I went up to him and turned on my flashlight. Between his two front paws was a plastic water bottle that looked new. I gave him a verbal reward and told him to track again. He continued on the track, following the scent sidehill, and then turned down the mountain – pulling the leash hard. All of a sudden, he stopped and started barking at something ahead of us in the bushes. I turned on my light and could barely see a man in a jacket, lying on his stomach in the bushes, not 30 yards out in front of us. I gave the person multiple orders to show us his hands. When he didn't comply, I sent Karma in to apprehend him so that no officers would be harmed if he tried to use the knife.

Karma did his job. He ran down and took a big bite. He had a big mouthful of the person's jacket and began pulling as hard as he could, which rolled the man onto his side. I could see that his hands were empty. The assault suspect was quickly put in handcuffs by the deputies and hauled off to jail to face justice. Good boy K9 Karma!

Being the chief of police in the City of Republic was one of the highlights of my life. I had made it my life's mission to stand up for law and order. Protecting the good citizens, their rights, and the rights of criminals went hand in hand. As much as I detested the actions of some criminals, I always made it a point to pass on some wisdom and hope to them as I was hauling them off to jail. Some heeded the words, and I never saw them in handcuffs again. Some didn't, and became "frequent flyers."

One thing I know after being a police officer for almost 11 years, and a chief of police for four, is that the thin blue line must be protected. We have to honor our police officers. They are what stand between the law-abiding and total mayhem. We have to strongly reject the socialists who are calling to defund the police. I've said it many times, but it bears repeating, and I hope you agree with me: defunding the police is the stupidest thing I've ever heard of.

Some would like to convince us that the police are bad, that they are a bunch of racist killers, that the mere sight of a black person incites rage inside of a police officer, and that they can't control the urge to just pull out their gun and shoot a person down . . . so, therefore, we need to defund them. While I do believe that law enforcement is under tremendous pressure to deal with criminals, drug addicts, and highly stressful situations, day-in and day-out, race isn't a deciding factor when it's time to use deadly force. The criminal's activity and the officer's perceived threat in that moment is the deciding factor.

I also understand that it takes a community of skilled professionals that work together to not only stop the offenses, but to help prevent repeat offenses through mental health counseling and effective drug addiction programs. I highly recommend the book *Cop Under Fire* by David Clarke, which talks about some of these very important issues. The author presents critical facts and opinions that can help us all move forward together with truths that are not readily available in the mainstream media. The book is available on Audible as well.

In that book, Sheriff Clarke breaks down the actual events that have made headlines all across this nation and details the truth that most in the media and the far-left radical race-baiters skim over. If a white cop shoots a black person, they are immediately deemed a racist by some; no further evidence needed. That is unacceptable. If we are concerned about people being killed, and we darn sure should be, there are many ways to bring awareness to the problem that truly exists in inner cities and beyond.

There are cities like Chicago where 20 to 40 people of color are shot every week by other people of color. Black-on-Black crime is a significant problem. And, police officers who are trying to keep the peace and enforce the law, without bias regarding the race of the perpetrator, are not a factor in this issue. We need to come together as Americans, no matter what our race is, and stop the division being instigated by those who profit from it – the media, politicians, Jesse Jackson, Al Sharpton, and anyone else who ignores the facts.

Together, we can create a more unified and peaceful world where the law is enforced and people of all races feel safe in their homes and communities. That will not come from eliminating police officer positions, nor from saying that every shooting is about race – when it clearly is not, once the facts come out.

CHAPTER SIXTEEN

Remember when I told you about my experience in Korea during Team Spirit '83, when our convoy drove through those little villages and everyone who lived there came out to the street to greet us? They didn't care what race the soldiers in the trucks were. They went out of their way to show us love and appreciation, because we were Americans! The color of our skin didn't matter to them; the only thing that mattered was the nation we came from, and what we stood for as Americans. We freed their country during the Korean War, and we were there to protect them from the communist threat from the north. That's what mattered; that's why they waved. That's why they smiled, and that's why they waved our nation's flag. We need to remember that here at home. We are all part of one nation, we are all part of one race, and that is the HUMAN RACE.

One of the things that I did as police chief that garnered a lot of unintended attention is when I made the public statement that I would not enforce an anti-gun initiative that passed in Washington State. Our socialist, anti-American Attorney General deceived most people in my state by giving a deceptive title to Initiative 1639. The title was all about gun and school safety, but inside the 30 pages was anti-American, anti-Constitutional garbage. I took an oath of office three times in my public life: in the military, when I became a police officer, and when I was promoted to chief of police. In that oath, that many of you may have taken as well, it says, "I will uphold and defend the Constitution." I meant it when I took that oath, and when that initiative passed, I publicly said I would not enforce it.

In the Washington State Constitution, in Article 1, Section 24, it says: "The right of the individual citizen to bear arms in defense of himself or the state shall not be impaired." That is very plain language, and I was not going to violate my oath of office. That stance made national news. I did not know that a public servant, which I was, standing up for citizens' rights was national news, but I quickly found out it was. I did interviews with Tucker Carlson, NRA-TV, One America News Network, and I was quoted in hundreds of newspaper and radio interviews from all over the United States. That interest, and the lack of other law enforcement executives standing up for the citizens they work for, led me to write what would become a best-selling book, *American Cop*.

In that book, I made the case for the Constitution and citizens' rights, and how all public servants have a duty to stand up for their oath of office. I wrote that entire book in the month of December 2018, and when it was published in early 2019, it went to No. 1 on Amazon in three different categories. To my amazement, it was soon the No. 1 best-selling book on the Hot 100 new books list on Amazon, and it stayed at No. 1 for multiple weeks! Obviously, people were hungry for the truth, and it wasn't coming from the nightly news or most politicians.

I was soon speaking at Republican Party Lincoln Day Dinners all over the state, and was a guest speaker at many sportsman's shows and gun shows. Almost every weekend during the spring, and into the summer of 2019, I was traveling somewhere speaking about our rights, our responsibilities, and the importance of ensuring we the people make our public servants – known as politicians – stand up for our rights and uphold and defend the Constitution. All the while, I maintained my full-time position as police chief of Republic.

More and more people started reading *American Cop*. As I traveled the state, week in and week out, more and more people started coming to these events . . . and then people started asking me to run for governor. Being a politician was the furthest thing from my mind. Being in the public eye, on national TV, and at speaking events were not things I had planned to do. I was not a public speaker; in fact, I hated public speaking. I wasn't good at it, nor did I have a desire to do it. Most of the time, I'd break out in a sweat when I had to get in front of anyone and say anything (I still do sometimes), but someone had to do it, and I wasn't going to back down from the challenge.

As time went on into the summer of 2019, I could not ignore the number of people who were saying the same thing. No matter where I went, I was hearing, "Will you run for governor?" or "We need you as governor," or "We need someone who will stand up for the Constitution."

In July of 2019, I had a serious talk with my wife Barb about what people were asking me to do. It wasn't something that I took lightly, especially since Barb had some previous health issues with brittle bones that had caused her vertebrae to fracture multiple times. She required three different surgeries on her back over the past few years. She also had a tumor removed from her lung the year prior, and was having some short-term memory problems that nobody could figure out.

She encouraged me to run for the sake of our state and our grandchildren's future, so we made the decision to do it. Then the questions in my mind began to take on reality. *How will I do it? Will anyone support a small-town country boy from the middle of nowhere? How will I raise money? I'm jumping into a big pond; will I even make a ripple?*

I didn't know the answers to these questions. I just knew that, once again, I wanted to do the right thing no matter what. I knew that someday, when I reached the end of my life's road, I would be taking my last breath and having my last thought. I didn't want that thought to be, *You really should have tried . . .*

Loren campaigning with Barb

Acknowledgments

To our Creator, the God of the universe. Thank you for this life and the many struggles and blessings in it; thank you for the forgiveness through our savior Jesus Christ.

To my wife, Barb – for over 43 years, you have been by my side. You are a blessing to me, sent from God above to help guide me through this experiment called life. Without you, I would be less than half the man I am.

To my family, who has helped shape who I am and who have always been there for me, especially my brothers, Randy, Kevin and Wade. I'll see you around the campfire.

The free and independent citizens who think for themselves, those who don't mind taking a risk and are always ready to defend our way of life as our country's founders, and God, intended. I thank you all... we aren't done... we aren't alone... buckle up... "Let's do what we do." YOU have inspired me!

April O'Leary and the entire crew at O'Leary Publishing, thank you for being true professionals. I consider you all friends. You have done an amazing job.

One quick note to my grandchildren, Isabella, Hyde, Araceli, Sy'rai, Ruger, Charlie, Jackson, and Gracie Mae. No matter what life throws at you, never, ever give up! There will be good times and bad times, but look at each chapter in your life as a learning experience; always challenge yourself. Don't ever be afraid to step out of your comfort zone. Always stand up for what's right, never back down, and forever strive to be the best person that you can be. You literally can be, and do, anything you set your mind to. I love you all!

About the Author

Loren Culp is the #1 best-selling author of American Cop: Upholding the Constitution and Defending Your Right to Bear Arms. His viral Facebook post in November 2018 threw him into the national media spotlight for his defense of the Second Amendment as a Police Chief in Republic, WA. That led to his first book and book tour, which led to his statewide campaign for Governor in 2020. He garnered the most votes for any Republican candidate in Washington State history.

Loren has been married to his wife Barb for 43 years and they currently live in Republic. He is the father of two sons and Grandfather of 8. For more information about Loren, to order autographed copies of his books and for patriotic gear please visit www.chiefculp.com. You can also watch his weekly Live show "Common Sense with Chief Culp" on the Chief Loren Culp YouTube channel every Tuesday evening

CPSIA information can be obtained
at www.ICGtesting.com
Printed in the USA
FSHW011451010421

9 781952 491139